INTERCITY FLOW

an international anthology

edited by
Andy Willoughby & Bob Beagrie

EK ZUBAN

First published September 2015
by Ek Zuban
c/o 52 Carlow Street
Middlesbrough
TS1 4SD
United Kingdom
www.ekzuban.org.co.uk
andy_ekzuban@hotmail.com

EK ZUBAN

ISBN: 978-0-9572807-7-9

Edited by Bob Beagrie & Andy Willoughby
Assistant Editor — Laura Forbes

All photographs courtesy of Kevin Howard
http://www.kevhowardcreativephotography.com/
Except for the photograph of Bob Beagrie -
courtesy of Jess Watson
jess_watson@ymail.com

Cover and design by Bob Beagrie

Printed by Evoprint & Design Ltd,
2 Simcox Court, Riverside Park
Middlesbrough, TS2 1UX
sales@evoprintanddesign.co.uk

This publication has been made possible through the support of
Arts Council England, Teesside University
Redcar & Cleveland Borough Council,
The Danish Arts Foundation, The Dutch Embassy and Runoviikko

Table of Contents

The Intercity Flow

Throughout 2014 - 2015 Ek Zuban Press ran a ground breaking poetry mentoring project involving Teesside, London, Avignon, Den Haag, Copenhagen and Turku. Well established poets/spoken word artists, who are all involved in literary activism and live promotion, mentored emerging younger poets in writing, performance and project delivery—culminating in a high voltage programme of shows at Teesside's legendary Electric Kool-Aid Cabaret at Redcar's Tuned In Centre and a book launch at the London Literature Festival 2015.

This anthology contains work from older and younger poets from each city, offering readers a rare chance to see contemporary poetics at play across Europe and the U.K. and to consider the relationship between page and performance, poet and society.

It was exciting to share good practice, to allow new networks to evolve between all of the poets and refreshing to see Teesside developing further as a focal point where national and international poetics meet, extending the area's reputation as a unique centre for poetic activity, following the first T-Junction International Poetry Festival in 2014.

The young poets on the project shared creative writing walks from Middlesbrough to Saltburn, assisted in workshops with school children and university students, attended symposiums, experienced working in collaboration with live musicians, performed both live and on film at Teesside University's state of the art media centre, and received one to one support. The senior poets were able to compare working practice, engage in translation and explore future collaborations with an emphasis on poetry projects with a social impact, and to share in the richness of the landscape, heritage and culture of Teesside, with its long standing live literature scene and small press tradition, its contrasting scenery of post-industrial city-scape, its dramatic coast with towering cliffs, long beaches and its rugged moorlands and hills, helping to contradict the narrow stereotyping of the area.

The Intercity Flow Anthology provides a cosmopolitan snapshot of spoken and written word across cultures and linguistic boundaries. The live cabaret events were multi-lingual although this book only has space for the English versions, we hope the poets in each country will offer further versions in their own languages. It was a privilege to be involved in a pan-European project with creative people that proved the value of a multi-cultural approach and shows how we are all so much bigger together in an age where there is growing pressure towards a narrow isolating nationalism.

Bob Beagrie & Andy Willoughby
Ek Zuban Press & Literature Development

EK ZUBAN

Bob Beagrie

A widely published poet across the U.K. & Europe. His publications include *The Seer Sung Husband* (Smokestack Press), *Glass Characters* (Red Squirrel Press), *KIDS* (Mudfog) and *SAMPO: Heading Further North*—written with Andy Willoughby (Red Squirrel Press). His next collection, *Leasungspell* will be published by Smokestack in 2016. His work has appeared in numerous anthologies and magazines and has been translated into numerous languages. He is a Senior Lecturer at Teesside University, works on social and educational projects with Ek Zuban and is a founding member of the experimental music and spoken word experiment Project Lono

https://soundcloud.com/projectlono-1

No one spoke of the cloud

though Marie played dutifully on the pianoforte
and sang, and somebody complemented her voice,
"Exquisite" was one word used, another
Was "Unearthly".

We ate. We drank.
When Sophia laughed she gave an involuntary little snort
that took her, and Claude, by surprise,
but no one spoke of the cloud.

It was a foggy, damp old day to begin with.
Mist hung heavily in the grounds
but the cloud on the lawn was whiter,
starker, more alien, spreading

quite disturbingly beneath
the conversation which acknowledged
the flock wallpaper, Lady Dampier's ball gown
Phillip's new purebred and how all the children grow.

While the cloud unfurled like a pallid octopus in tissue paper
locked into a silent skirmish with itself, until
thankfully it appeared to strangle itself
and the trails and fronds drifted away
toward the damp trees and the ornamental lake,

and, fortunately, no one thought it necessary
nor reasonable to mention it.

Stray City

Live jazz plays
through the warm city evening,
cobbles shine with lamplight from soft cafes
ashimmer on canal water,
you follow the feet of the beat,
transferred from venue to venue,
from speaker to speaker
over bridges arched like turtle shells
adrift, far from home -
far from home among restless crowds
who seem to own a sense of place,
of purpose,
with bearings stamped in lanes of feeling
on the inside of eyelids;
joking at tables,
offloading the day,
just watch the hours vanish,
ice cubes in cocktail glasses.

Opposite the Kirk
an upstairs window aglow
with lamps: orange, red and pearl,
a tube of bulbs around a mantle –
a grotto, although
no one inside is visible
from the street. How tempting
to knock
and enquire who dressed
the window
in such a homely fashion,
but you have a long journey ahead
and suspect a siren,
a witch, a gorgon
while the laureates of stone ledges

coo from the Gutter of Prophesy.

Later in Harry's attic
on Jacob Catstraat you dream
of the sea, white-linen ripples
trailing smooth boards and you –
an earwig adrift in the corner
of a cabin of a ship wreck; waves
of distant drum beats, rhythm-rushes
of panic, calm, panic, calm,

just as you are, stretched
upon a mattress
like Gregor Samsa, watching
six stringy limbs scrabble at air,
clutching for something solid
while from somewhere,
streets away night sirens wail.

Searim Seiðr

(Dróttkvætt)

Turbines tear at skylines
Stitched together by gulls
Fret weaving on wing-lift,
We watch one another

As ghosts weather-grounded
Grappling with apple dreams,
We hoard safe the heart-seeds
Hands held up to heaven.

River ripened verses,
Vacuum wrapped rune visions
Re-sung with the blood's drum;
Draw crow days in coal-dust

Song-bound to the singers:
Spiral of a sea shell
Tide marooned rockpools
Recall last wave's caress.

Evening wends homeward,
Hauls Night in its keep-net,
To warm flesh by firelight,
Faces dance in flame-tongues.

Wild eyes watch the crackle
Creeping embers crumble
Knife-edge draws Night's gullet
Gather round, my Goslings.

Believe that you belong,
Become strong as iron -
Feed full on Night's carcass
Keep its bones for relics.

Settle down for slumber,
Sleep shall send us stalking
Along seams of starways
Searching for the morning.

Will Dixon

William Michael Dixon currently resides in his home town of Hartlepool, and has been involved with the Intercity Flow Project since 2014. He has performed at several Electric Kool-Aid Cabaret events and Cabaret TS24, in Hartlepool. Dixon is also a writer of short stories as well as poetry, specialising in the genres of Horror and Science-Fiction. Currently studying English Studies at Teesside University he hopes to pursue a career in the film and comic book industries after graduation.

"Will is a very promising young writer whose work has a social bite, and he is not afraid to play with both private and public voices as well as using narrative ventriloquism to explore personae within his poems. While rooted firmly in the real world his interest in Sci-Fi and Horror gives his poetry an undercurrent of otherworldliness. He has great stage presence and throughout the mentoring period it has been a pleasure to see his confidence, abilities and understanding of form develop."

Bob Beagrie

Walk Beyond It and Find Out

Skeletal trees crown the horizon.
Guarding the garden is a white, stone lion.
The constant cooing of pigeons
the hammering of tools from Dad's shed.
A frog in the pond lurches itself across the water.
In the garden I see the archaic voice of time:
the old Sun Dial. A stone statue
Is obscured by manicured hedges.
Autumn is coming, the leaves vacate their branches.
I know that my Dad killed a colony of rats
beneath the conservatory. Is there a secret
garden between the hedges?
Walk beyond it and find out.
Walk beyond it and find out…
I wish I didn't have those nightmares.
Dad shouts me down for tea, startling me
into a sense of clear vision and normality.

Liberty's Children

Our captors are talking amongst themselves again,
Deciding how they should play out our fate,
Like an old childhood board game,
That we always lost.

Promises lined with words spoken with smooth venom,
Bred to hate and exploit, to lie and to deceive
To close our third eye that lets us perceive the world as we wish,
To sour our words of freedom with the stench of war.
Can you feel the effect of this dome placed over our heads?
See the smoke of their damage emblazoned in our horizons,
Yet they sit and smile at the chaos.
Organised confusion rains down upon us,
Like tar seeping from the eyes of an iron monstrosity.

You can't see through the visor placed before you
Shielding your view of reality.
Are the puzzles of life and death,
Just a mere misconception?
What do I label 'real' or 'fantasy'
In a world where reality is the stuff of monsters
Dressed in suits and bathed in power?
Where dreams are grown on mighty stalks
Only to have the heads of the flowers harvested before us
Out of fear of our dreams becoming uncontrollable.
They don't want our dreams
To become their reality.

The lambs are dying
The sun is no longer shining upon us

For we are not worthy of its radiance -
        So we are told...

The fields of our labour
The fruits of our minds
Are run down and torn apart
Like the rabbit from the hunt.

We hang limp from the clenched jaws of politicians
As the pack in the distance whistles and barks -
The noise drowns us like chill waves of the North Sea
Filling our lungs, our mouths, our hearts.

The ticking hours of the clock push forward,
The working man and woman push onward,
The dreams of the united stand still
Not daring to move, not wishing to be disturbed.
Are we truly entitled to liberty?

Sharks Washed Down in Whiskey

Sometimes I feel
so shit about myself
that I want to throw my insides up
and start again, fresh.

Maybe if I stopped
moving forwards
I might cease up and rust
and float, aimlessly.

I could turn off my mind
and separate it
from my pathetic excuse of a body
that I abuse, endlessly.

I could stop
anytime I want to
but I don't, I continue onwards
my eyes open, waiting.

I should sit down
take the weight away
from my heavy clothed feet
that stand there, supporting.

I'll open my mouth
and pour within it
a thousand and one sorrows
golden flow, bittersweet.

I can feel it
trapped and entwined
around my gut like a rope

the anchor hangs, dragging.

Mace tears
rolling down
burning and cooling
my throat tenses, scratching.

The atmosphere's thick
around my head
like a heavy, lead crown
the brain cries, throbbing.

Crystal fogs
clouds dampen
I can hear, but
I can't move, drowning.

Siddhartha Bose

Siddhartha Bose's books are *Kalagora* and *Digital Monsoon* (Penned in the Margins) He has been featured on BBC 4, BBC Radio 3 and dubbed one of the 'ten rising stars of British poetry' by *The Times*. He performs internationally in spellbinding dramatic multi media renderings of his work.

Sid's plays include *Kalagora*, acclaimed at Edinburgh Fringe 2011, *London's Perverted Children*, long-listed for an Oxford Samuel Beckett Theatre Trust award, and *The Shroud*. His book on the grotesque is *Back and Forth* and his film, *Animal City*, is in competition at the Goa Short Film Festival 2015. Siddhartha has been a Leverhulme Fellow in Drama and has guest-edited an issue of *Wasafiri* on international urban writing.

More at: www.kalagora.com

Prelude

In your life, you—fortunate Caliban—dreamt of fair England, green.

In your death, I whisper to you in a dark basement room, in a narrow lane, by Shoreditch and Curtain Road.

2008, January.

On the streets, piss-pools lather chipped pavements. Bars explode. Phantoms trade in the dark's orange glow.

All around, empty warehouse matchboxes. Wax paintings on broken walls. Lonely beggars with torn bleeding arms.

In this aged set, made-up revellers hide blank noise.

~~

My room, a litter of smoke, black magic artefacts.

A small, dust-covered TV.

A double mattress on the floor.

A single yellow streetlamp.

Cloth-cupboards with squealing mice.

A black stain on the floor, for a sofa.

A black guitar with a broken E string.
Two mirrors—cracked—reflecting each other.

Maps and blackn'white photographs of Kolkata (the view from the balcony, where you waved goodbye—telephone wires, yellow cabs, monsoon streets) on the wall.

In this cave—banished light—my bones slip, skin falls, ghosts become.

~~

I tell you Shakespeare—negative-capability-blood-man—lived round the corner. Marlow lived up the road, edging Hackney.

Four hundred years ago, this scab of the city lay beyond the puritan fathers.

It's still the same. A web of death, ghosts, sex, stretched tragic masks.

A city of closed windows, drawn curtains, plague-memories.

The Book of the Dead

In a stale Victorian house that
houses the dead in London, mother

tells me you came to her in a dream. You'd
written a book, she says, a history of the

dead, like you always wanted to.

You were showing it off to your friends, your peers,
proud as the parent you were, or wanted to be,

progenitor of speech. Rust-voiced.

~~

The book is in your hands, and it is
red leather and the smell of ink is cutting.

Your hands trem-
ble and

                    fall like the
                    sudden

                    drop of a kite, or a

                              plane in air-pockets.

~~

In a memory that visited mother like

an oracle, warning of dust and bones,
the dying gods — like healing wounds —

strike you down again. In your passion, she says,

your heart becomes a bomb in a Navajo desert.
Explodes. A thousand suns.

Mother wakes up, joyous she glimpsed
you again. In sepia. While you

die — again —
dry up, like the liquid of the dream that
carried you to her — a magic lantern
        floating on
                cancered water.

Peace

A holy beard-
man by the river
with a stick
begging
gray diseased water
gray sky
Howrah bridge in the distance
like a gigantic spider
straddling the river
Jain temples
the priest chanting
before the funeral
I sleep with a friend
when I come
my back
splits in
two
I exhale my
father's
breath
Om
shantih
shantih
shantih

Will Tyas

A former member of the Barbican Young Poets, Will Tyas is a London based artist and member of the Burn After Reading Collective. Will has performed at Ronnie Scott's Jazz Club; had theatrical works performed in London; collaborated on "Unleashed" with Barbican Guildhall and composed poetry soundtracks for artists such as Joelle Taylor and Antosh Wojcik.

"A remarkable young poet, Will Tyas is equally comfortable on stage and page. His work has variety and draws on his many interests and areas of expertise like music and performance. As a spoken word artist and performer, his style is engaging and effortless. On the page, Tyas' writing is sharp, spare, funny and weird in a way that illuminates and arrests the reader. There is depth and quality here, and an emerging voice that is unique and generous."

Siddhartha Bose

Find him on Twitter: @willtyas

The Sinking of the Titanic

Bring me back The Night when you go home.
Drag the folded circus tent cross country.
The bodily weight of the cosmos swings
with the circuitry of your tiny arms.

Both of your feet are shivering
and the red army shot their own men
at Stalingrad. Here I go again.
Colouring you in with TV static.

I could be wrong about everything.
The hulking left hand of a bass player
makes pianos into murder weapons.
Everything melts and you just get taller.

Here we go again. I'm drawing
cataracts into magazine photos
because my grandmother lives in rainclouds.
Here I go again. The hand that holds

my house keys twitches over the Thames
and your shivering mini fist
is holding keys in the crooks of fingers
and their sharp ends are sniffing the air.

We unzip the sky in this tiny room
and in the fullness of yawning dark
the stars are playing each other.
Listen. Feet shiver. Hands shake.

A Fear of Staircases

Mum was listening
hard to the floor.
Ear to the ground.
Feet at difficult
angles.

In a totem pole.
Grave stone coloured.
I haul life upstairs
in fruit boxes.

In a satellite town
of a satellite town
mum was upside down
an upended tree.

A strings cut puppet
was hauled onto stairs
and red cleaned off
and airwaves cleared.

I carry movies
upstairs about
tragedies & families
and time melts wax

around my twitching
fingers that ache
with dragging a life
beside motorways.

She slinkied downstairs
foot over skull
　　and came to rest to
listen to the floor.

                              I am listening
                          hard to the floor
                                  in the flat that
                          my mum hasn't seen

          and every staircase
          and every hard floor
          in a totem pole
          in a satellite town

          is echoing with
          the sound of falling.
Thank Christ. She is still breathing.

In the Back of a Cab with Aisling

I admit to snorting powdered
secrets until my nose bleeds.
This will happen whether
you want it to or not.

I love the way the air tastes
clean and cold like mint
but refuses to take on colour.
You have hung blackout

curtains. The stars are
sneaking up in gangs.
One million suns jostle for
position in a dynamite sky.

Everything that happens
will happen now.
Aeroplanes are skimming like
empty shoes on lakes.

Jetsam souls sink until the sea
is so full you could walk it.
Everything will eventually
compact and turn to stone.

Eventually we will snort
painkillers until nothing
isn't grey or damp or soft
in attack and decay.

Until our DNA stretches
out into flat ladders
that we can fax and
re-helix later somewhere else.

Eventually your nose will
bleed tympani skin.
You will pull bed sheets
from your aching throat.

Eventually air will take
the shape of what it
sees the most. The
rest will turn to stone

Eventually these islands will
turn dark as leaf litter.
This will happen whether
we want it to or not.

Eventually the sky will expand
like dough and press us against
the planet. Gasping like dead fish.
I have never admitted to bleeding

litres into a sink or to
wanting hands to fuse
like frozen lamp posts.
Have you ever been more

in love with everything than
when you haven't drowned?
When hands are burning
on fireworks and melting

together in prayer position.
More in love than when the
stars gang up and lift you
and fling you out to

the boiling obsidian sea
to drown in clean, mint, liquid sky.
All this will happen whether
we want it or not.

Esa Hirvonen

Esa Hirvonen (a.k.a Jesus of the Elk) is a legendary beat poet, shamanic traveller and one of the strongest and most original poetic voices of the Turku Poetry School. He has been a major force in The Flesh of The Bear Exchange with Teesside poets for fifteen years. He is a cult figure in the North East of England as well as in Finland.

Publications include *Harlem* (Savukeidas), a collection of palindromic poems: *Takana kapakan akat* (Savukeidas) and a collaborative chapbook with Jo Colley, *Punch Drunk* (Ek Zuban). Hirvonen cites Gregory Corso and Dan Fante as influences for his third full collection, *Uralin nälkä*. His poetics involve clashing classical language with the hard discourse of modern reality. His poetry has been translated into English, Estonian, Udmurt, Slovenian and Italian. As well as being a poet/performer, he is chairman of Runoviikko: Poetry Week Association of Southwest Finland. He was the City Artist for Turku between 2014 – 2015

www.burningbridge.fi/authors/esa-hirvonen/

Aiyeh Leh

Oh England your lost empire, Indian spice trade,
liao lah, all the long gone gods, Liverpool hits
stones of Stonehenge have seen a lot, still staying stoned,
where are your prophets now?
they speak singlish now lalalaa and long for curry,
manglish they sing shilalaa

Oh Celts, Eires, when the greatest of Anglo-Saxons, David Beckham scores
and walks alone, what happens to the language, fish and chips,
oh Ireland your potatoes and independence, stout and black Irish,
who threw the first bomb, oh me who so self sure studied your language
should have stopped psychedelics back then o'reddy: heresceafta heap?
Ic eom Hroðgares ar ond ombiht. Ne seah ic elþeodige!
þus manige men modiglicran, are the strangers in an odd mood...

Whatever they talk about in the London Underground, oysters with tabasco,
lemon or even mint jelly, Victoria Station by night, bum a dime, go North,
Beowulf orders kebab, a hundred thousand didgeridoos memorise your youth, oh-ha, oh
endless (Yorkshire pudding) green meadows and scary sheep,
beauty of the wool and this night, when we walk from the moors to Loftus,
whip girl waiting in The Shakespeare pub in Durham City, chains in my bag,
kil-kal, oh if this could all be just a dream, King of Denmark in Christiania
lies on strawberry fields and blueberry hills and does not think, aiyah,
cannot wait any no more, must go o'reddy.

Oh Hadrianus your spa lasted longer than your wall
and still they drink ale here, not Litina Barbera d´asti Superiore
and oh me, who is taken to the Lion and Parrot to sober up,
þus manige men modiglicran, all my loved ones, who have forgotten me,
aiyah, tape is running o'reddy, I'm recording on my back now,
Abbey Road is calling, must go o'reddy, what are we leaving behind us,
even the brave ones are afraid now, aiyah leh, gimme more drum,
'cause tonight I'll drink my last grand and return to Finland....

Greetings From Stockholm

You're so beautiful,
you bambieyed straightmouth
and together with the sun
beyond the wooden houses
reality disappears.

I cook for you: elk with cranberryvodka sauce
you throw the mighty bull out,
rather watch my cramps in the Dam &
my love for cloister beers in Brussels -
Delirium Tremens is my favourite label!

I drink all our money
with a Caribbean stripper,
call my ex to send more
& fill the bathtub with vomit.

You touch my hair and other bits
tell me what they said in hotel reception
THE GENTLEMAN IS WAITING IN THE BAR
we laugh and next time
I promise to be so good
strip for you and make food.

But again in Stockholm Esa the Elk
has to guzzle with Howard the Duck
and Crille the Crocodile in Prinsen,
sing old folksongs naked the whole night.

It could be so easy to call
this bohemian life
my own stupid circus.

In Boro Harbour
(On Kapoor's Temenos)

No ships, no workers, no steel,
old buildings getting older,
unemployment and broken football dreams,
there is nothing sacred in Boro harbour,
just an empty iron net's ghostly howling in the wind.

It is not a wormhole to the future,
where there is no Parmo, no stadium,
no red army shouting
Letś go fucking mental,
nah nah nah nah!

It is not a wormhole to an imaginary world,
where there is an old school bully as goalkeeper
and me scoring - Jari Litmanen style,
full stadium singing, *We are the Parmo army,*
Let´s go fucking mental

nah nah nah nah!

Temenos, a holy place is just a hole to a hole,
emptiness to emptiness,
there is nothing left for me to lose
in the Boro harbour.

Daniil Koslov

Daniil is a Russian-born poet from Turku, Finland. His style mixes punk, beat and experimental poetry, with black humour and existentialism. His latest collection was *Existence is a Nightmare of a Fairy Tale but at Least the Food is Kinda Okay*. His poetry and essays have been published in magazines, and he runs a small press: *Kolera*, focusing on underground, experimental poetry and anarchist literature. He also organizes events, translates poetry and teaches writing. His pseudonym "Susinukke Kosola" can be translated as Wolf Doll in Finnish.

"Daniil is one of the most promising poets in Finland, attracting the attention of many presses. His language skills are stunning and as a Turku poet his roots are deep in beat, underground, punk and anarchism. As well as mentoring him on this project, I have included him in Runoviikko projects in workshops with international poets and translated more obscure Fenn Ugrian languages like Mari into Finnish and English via Russian. He has taken much from this project."

Esa Hirvonen

Freedom

Every day is a choice:
How would you like to die today?

I've been killing myself like a poor man
bohemian babysteps and Bukowski's affirming words
yet it would still be more appealing
to die from a cuban cigar and not some cheap Bonus Gold rollups
but then again who knows
nicotine is still nicotine and tar
is just convenience food and that
is just another choice among others, a choice
to step into a mass grave & aluminium & plastic wrap

in to the same

the same bar's same walls
the many faces of the same ceilings and ninth-whiskey whirls
I don't think I can believe that some cheap Middlesbrough pub's ceiling
that's covered by old shipping boxes
is any better or worse or different(er)
and some people
die there and think
about the same whirls
in the squeaks of the ceiling fans
and they think about the Karlsson-on-the-Roof just like I do
when the head spins enough;
helikopteri, вертолёт, helicopter, IT ALL SPINS
LIKE A FUCKING MAD DOG CHASING ITS TAIL

A friend once told me
after interrailing all of Europe:
It's the same shit everywhere, just
in a different way.

And the freedom, yeah, it's the freedom
to choose your pub, its ceiling and walls and
yet we won't choose
because we've already chosen
each and every single day & evening & night
to be just like – to be just as much
as our freedoms allow us
and we don't know how to long for the scent of the Voronezh-village,
the smell of urine in St. Petersburg's elevators and the small pink sugarcube-buttons
next to them
the decomposing gluttony of Budapest

the law of conservation of energy,   entrophy,   a pub

and we miss the good days, the suicide
that left the smallest marks – no stitches at all!
But the concept of your own life
like it's felt or seen or whatever
when you feel the oxygen depleting and you still can't see the surface
and you wake up on the beach, between some stone walls & people & oxygen
you rise and go
to use your freedom in the nearest pub
that's a currency that's tied to luck, an idea

tied to self-deceit, and not

even to some vicious circle of it, but to a straight line

I wish I could remember why I live
even when I'm not about to die
but then again
I live
only because I'm yet not to.

Being Human

Being human, yeah,
after all
it's an experience that nobody remembers
after it's over
but

you can pet kittens that's
an essential part of being human nobody
else pets kittens or believes that
cats care
belief

that something bigger cares about us

something bigger sabotages us, something

no! everything belongs to us! because we are

people who pet kittens, who let their fingers
flow through the fur until
the cat's back starts to desertificate and erode
its mouth dries up and we're stroking a
body: that's an essential part of being human –
playing with the dead

Gunther von Hagen's made an exhibition
where he bent the dead into new life
for art
or at least he called it art
I guess that's a
part of being human

to look for a good way to die

just because he can't find a good way
to live
to pet the sky until it's dead to
plant couch potatoes for the farmer to pull up
gently by the umbilical cord
to enter the JOB MARKET
to attend WORK PARTIES
panties and genetalia petting is

being human is

a nonrecurring event like one night stands
in the parking lots of night clubs unless
you happen to believe in rebirth, but
even if you do
that's not always enough because
after all

everything important
only happens once.

Tomorrow we'll wake

when the Earth was flat we walked in circles
when the Earth became round we walked in rings
and the skyline tingled in our chests
as we followed the escaping flame with a sunstone
hoping for a philosopher's stone instead

and tomorrow we'll wake in utopia

when the Sun was a God we worshipped it
when the Sun became a star we burned in it
like deer in a forest fire galloping towards an Escape
these were the flames that melted Dali's clocks
and the hooves stuck in a sticky dream
as we hoped for the Truth

and tomorrow we'll wake in utopia

when Truth wore a capital letter we walked in circles
when truth shed its skin we walked in rings
lead weighed down our snowflakes
and we followed the escaping glow of radium
like a guttering olympic torch
hoping for a finish-line

after which
we would at least

ANDY WILLOUGHBY

Andy Willoughby is a poet and playwright from Middlesbrough and is a former Poet Laureate of the town. He has performed his work, often with musicians, across the U.K. and Europe. He works on social projects with Ek Zuban and has run a number of international poetry exchanges. He was a poetry coach for Apples & Snakes on The Word Cup and Shake The Dust projects. His latest collection is *Sampo: Heading Further North* (Red Squirrel Press) written with Bob Beagrie inspired by the Finnish *Kalevela*. He is also the author of *Tough* (Smokestack books), *Kids* (with Beagrie, Mudfog) and *The Wrong California: Middlesbrough Poet Laureate Poems* (Mudfog). He is a Senior Lecturer in Creative Writing at Teesside University. His next collection *Between Stations* – a long poem about travelling to Siberia with Finnish poets will be published by Smokestack Books in February 2016.

www.ekzuban.org.uk

For Vincent on the 125th anniversary of his suicide

Your letters to Theo, they kept me going
through the dish-washer, building site, hotel flunky years,
and when I was crunching grammar and usage for others
through night and day shifts most of them in those
ephemeral London shit-paid occupations;
"I come from Middlesbrough,
where do you come from?"
"I like football, I love my team
not Manchester United
because that is where I grew up,"
"Who is your team?"
"Where did YOU grow up?"
"I like books,
I am reading Van Gogh
and Milan Kundera -
Do you like the Unbearable Lightness of Being?"
"It was a good film yes, but the book is better."
The sunflowers in the National on rainy afternoons off:
the soul's luminosity and the dark seeds;
no more ridiculous for me to write
than for you to paint and get nowhere
in the material world, swapping absinthe for whisky,
scribbling notes and journals in one sink bedsits,
stinking of cabbage and labourers' socks,
with the punk neighbours screaming at each other
after too much cider, and still hanging on
to your notion of the dignity of the workers
and the possibilities of the quality of the light.

Four Kaukomieli Boys

On the road in one of Nik Nak's beat up bangers
This is it Amigos! Forget responsibility
The complications of home, work and family.
Swig on Jesus of the Elk's secret stash
Of sweet licorice-flavoured moonshine,
Become once more *The Blacklipped Bunch*,
Who know the meaning of a good time;
Suck slow on tins of last night's lager
Be the lightheaded lads of our own beat saga.
Let long Finn roads lined with birch and pine
Wash with flickering light four troubled minds

Oh these sweet mesmeric Tarmacced Lethe waters
Look out Tampere and Turku: Lock up your daughters!
Forget Ginsberg, Corso, Cassady and Kerouac
The 4 Kaukomieli horsemen are galloping back!
"We are the new Viikinki and we never miss a chance"
For a wild slam dance of word on wicked word -
Chanted and sung in ways you've never heard,
Chased down with smokie malt and the taste of a brawl,
We've got our motors running and we will never fall,
We'll speed like young heroes back up youth's highway
To Valhalla's hall and whatever comes our way.

Forget we are knocking on the door of 4 decades
We're Dylan's boys of summer impervious to age:
Now stop off and raid the Kaurismaki gas station,
Fill with suspect booty ramshackle chariot's boot
Roar off laughing like four feckless Lemminkainens:
Four Kaukomieli boys in a clown car backfiring!
Loaded up with fresh beer, giant bags of cheesie puffs,
And a retro Finn skin mag to make us feel tough -
Sexy Suvi Sings - a cut price sexline siren,
From sleek glossy pages with naked reader's wives in,
The only girls on tour we get to spend the night with.

We are the midsummer antidote to everything grey,
Four Bardic boys with the noise to blow your blues away,
Wringing out new notes from the old wizard's kantele.
Stick on a cheapo supermarket discount CD -
Greatest hits of Abba will sooth berserker rages,
Inspired by the disasters in all our back pages,
The sun won't set tonight but the road will take its toll
The Elk messiah slumps into a DT's backseat hole;
Dreams wood trolls are out to steal his fiery tongue,
Nick his blue light lyrics and seal his prophet's fate,
Four fuzzyheaded boys suddenly feel the weight.

Heavy shoulder burden of the lack of recognition
Second hand car stutters as Kalle floods the ignition,
We sit then weeping in a half-light layby state -
No longer able to throw off the minstrel's tragic fate
The sly nostalgic spell of jingling Benny and Bjorn
Has left us bereft, melancholy, time-torn;
Lonely and forlorn for our faraway lovers' touch -
The music drags us back as memories get too much
Agnetha leads four heroes like an evil white swan
Down through the deeps of too many lost days
To the cold black river through a summer heat haze.

At the raging cataract the illusion's torn to pieces
We're all empty handed with no golden fleeces,
Only slim volumes stand between us and oblivion
Though we all bravely declare we won't be giving in
And will yoik ourselves to wolves to make us strong
We know we are men who have sacrificed too long:
Hearts become stone on the day job's unforgiving altar
We've dropped the sacred sampo, let the grail quest falter:
Not young warriors but sad fathers of fast growing daughters,
Not four Kaukomieli boys ripe for the slaughter,
No, not light-headed boys still ripe for the slaughter.

The Wind in the Long Grass

That lion stalks my old man now;
its presence makes his feet drag,
turns his military gait into a shuffle.
His head's dropped imperceptibly,
shoulders weighed down
with my mother's absence
doing much more damage
than any weighted kit-bag.

Walking behind him in the country
I've got his back, and my eyes
are everywhere picking out
new blossoms and other sights
that will lighten his burden,
make him readier to fight
with all his ex-guardsman's might
if the pounce should come.

But you can't be there always
when you're a man yourself -
I get a call from my sister:
Dad's tripped, sprained his wrist
cracked and bruised a few ribs.
she tells me it was a paving stone
but I know he felt the creature
sniffing at his heels and stumbled.

As he recovers, stretches and trains
I implore the relentless beast :
please leave him alone a while yet,
though we both know he's yours;
allow us some more half marches;
since he put up his defences to you
he has finally dropped the walls
he built against me knowing him

all those straight-backed years.

Laura Anne Rea Tilbrook

Laura is a recent graduate of Teesside University's MA: Creative Writing. She is currently working on a poetry collection which explores noir and surrealist voices in local settings which she began developing during her time on the MA. She has since performed her poetry at various local venues and hopes to return to her work on a murder-mystery novel. Updates about her works in progress and upcoming poetry performances can be found on her Facebook page:

https://www.facebook.com/LauraTilbrookWriting

"Laura is a poet with a sharp eye and an ability to portray character and narrative in a few startling lines, her work has a mysterious elegant quality but bristles also with social observational details that have real visceral aspects. It was good working with her on the page and stage as she developed her urban noir miniatures and honed them to the absolute nitty gritty, employing her musical ability working with the Electric Kool Aid Cabaret's pianist The Amazing Mr.Flint to finalise the pieces through dedicated work in precise performance, She has a whole collection of these up her sleeve now."

Andy Willoughby

Park Lovers

Greasy tracksuits embark
upon today's methadone marathon
while caged artists lounge,
too relaxed for their depicted revolutions.
Two bar-fight faced men
push a pale blue pram
filled with gurgles and wide eyes
that watch another child,
with unusual accompaniment,
being chased by boombox boys
waving limbs.
Harassing mother and child
is a new art form.
A girl with lollipop hair,
strawberry and vanilla swirl,
stares at another pairing.
"Make sure you look after
that tracksuit" he shouts.
Electric mumblings vibrate in the breeze.
Valentine's Day is over,
now begins the dark Valentine's Night.

Cut

And he's off
on the crest of a heartbreak
down to the shop
for nailbreak tinnies
to serve as a
shop-close timewaster.

Daylight spent waiting
for scissor cuts to turn
to boxing glove punches.
Perfecting the hair of
Self-appointed Selfie Queens.

Time to step into the ring
without the one on his finger.
he squares up to walls
then swaggers home
with blood bruised knuckles.

He cries rivers to his wife
fishing for forgiveness, which
she grants him after
a half day's divorce.

Back to the salon of
contorted mirror frames
where he stares at his
animal reflection.
Punch turning to cut
as the first customer
walks in.

Wedding Ring

The ring strangled
my dutifully wed finger for
forty years before I broke
the bond that the band
held me to.
A static release in a
perfect moment.
I wondered how easily
the knife would sink into
flesh, like into butter or tar
or even perhaps the Sunday
Dinner - Roast Husband
stewed in the bitter juices
of sex arguments.
Instead, I turned it on myself -
the real victim.
staring at that gilded lump
of wrinkles on the counter
between us, he makes no move
to stem the blood from
flowing out of me and into
this butchered pig of a marriage.

Joelle Taylor

Poet, award winning playwright and author with over 15 years' experience of working in schools, colleges and universities. A former UK slam champion, she founded the national youth slam championships SLAMbassadors in 2001. She has performed her poetry nationally and internationally for the British Council – including Zimbabwe, Botswana, 100 Club, Trafalgar Square, the 02 Arena, Royal Court, Buckingham Palace, Pentonville Prison and on a pontoon in the middle of the North Sea. Her collection *Ska Tissue* (Mother Foucault Press) is in its 4th edition, and a new collection *The Woman Who Was Not There* (Burning Eye Books) Her novel *(W)horror Stories* is due for publication in 2016. She has written a chapter about the transformative effect of spoken word in a new poetry pedagogy text *Making Poetry Happen* published by Bloomsbury. She has featured on radio and television. She has been added to the OCR English syllabus for 2015, and will be touring the UK over 2015 and 2016 in a new one woman spoken word show *The Space Between Words*. She was recently awarded a Change Maker prize, awarded annually in recognition of work that changes lives, given on behalf of Nelson Mandela Trust. She is the host of the Southbank Centre's National Poetry Day: LIVE.

http://slam.poetrysociety.org.uk. http://joelletaylordotorg.wordpress.com

Ansisters

These vagabond women
These wrong haired girls
These walkers along Fallopian roads that curve into names
These sisters of broken teeth
Derelict terraces in the rubble of mouths
These flocks of shrieks
These punched laughs
These clutched keys
These copywriters of bed sheets
These rouges of bruises
These deep nights of ugly and beauty and innocence
See how we birthed the word.
See how we unpicked razor wire perimeters like badly knitted jumpers
See the smiles scarring our faces
See how we dreamed in different languages
See how we cradled suffragettes in the soft of our fists
See how we danced at the end of the world.
See how we lived in hard houses
See the chill out that kept us warm
See the storm at the edges of eyes
See the thin line we stepped over
And inhaled
And wore as hangmen's ropes around our necks
See the stain on the wall turn into the face of your mother
See her smoking
See her clean herself into corners
See her wash herself away
See her rubbed out
Haunting you from your polished boots
See brown girls pirouetting from umbilical ropes
Strung from the old man's hand of a stripped yew tree
See a picnic at the end of the world

See our gingham grins
See a land beneath a single bed
See women invaded like oil rich countries
See two mouths. Neither of them speaking.
See white girls written over
See black women
See black women
See black women
See the presence of absence
See the woman sewn inside her father
See the child tap dance in a gilded bird cage
See women flicker like neon lights
See a girl catch a bullet in her teeth. And swallow.
See an army of Russian Dolls stretching behind and before you
See infinity.

These vagabond women
These wrong haired girls
Who held hands when you could not
And sang songs you had forgotten the words to
And carried you. Carried you.

Our Ansisters
Hold them to the light
On clear nights:
You can see yourself.

A Human Writes
(commissioned by Apples and Snakes as an Alternative Magna Carter)
'For too long, we have been passively tolerant society, saying to our citizens 'as long as you obey the law we will leave you alone'' David Cameron, British Prime Minister
'They tried to bury us. They forgot we were seeds' Mexican Proverb

Let us build our homes from our ancestors' bones
Let us speak
Let our names never be too heavy for our tongues to lift
Let no brick wall
Spittle statute graffitied
Divide any kiss
Let our palm prints be maps that lead us to each other
Let us argue.
Let us agree.
Let no government decree delivered from a chattering TV absolve us of collective responsibility
Let the traveller walk.
Let us melt guns with the heat of our breaths
And mould the molten metal in to
School desks. Hospital beds.
Into butterflies
Let us stand together and watch them rise and re-write the blank skies
Let them become confetti
That blesses every union.
Let us sometimes be wrong.
Let us never use our tongues as overseers' whips
Let us pay reparations. Let us remember.
Let us clear a space on the sofa for you. Let me cook a soup for you in my language.
Let us bake bread.
Let us read.
Let us teach.
Let us stand on top of tower blocks and preach the sermons of free speech
Let us not snap hearts like communion wafers
Let her cover her face
Let us bite through umbilical chains that bind sex trafficked slaves
Let no woman be taught how to walk

Let no man be pushed from a roof as though gravity were his lover
Let us remember the legend of our wings
Let us summon the hidden things
Let us unfold our skins and write peace treaties on them
Let us speak
Let us translate our pot-bellied lives into pixels
Let us roam free across unchartered digital worlds
Let my door be a door.
Let us breathe.
Let us believe
In whatever God is not too busy to listen
Let us open the windows of our prisons
Let them howl rainbows.
Let no lip be sewn
Vaginal or oral
Let the electoral system put the people in power
Let the Pound Shops be Parliaments
The corner shops seats of government
Let us have a House of Whores.
Let us not post our votes into ballot boxes as though they were coffins
Let us be dissident. Resilient. Difficult to train
Let us declare ourselves innocent
Until proven guilty
Let us be imperfect
Let us be tolerant
Let the land remember the rain
Let the soil remember the seed
Let us tear down fences and use them to construct bridges
Let us open our borders
Like the arms of a mother
We have been waiting for you
Let her not carry the war in her womb
Let us sing out of tune
Let us not march to our drum but dance
Let every smile be a curve in the road
Let us wonder what comes next
Let us wonder

Let us hold hands with someone we are afraid of
Let us hold hands with ourselves
Let our school children teach
One lesson a week each
Let the origami girls unfold
Let the standing boys sit down
Let us eat
Let us pay each other in poetry
Let us make town square fires
Tumbling pyres of burning money
Let us place our fingers to the lips, the total eclipse, of gun barrels
Hush now. We are dreaming
Let us understand that every town has its Palestine
Every home has its Gaza
Let our headlines not be epitaphs
Our televisions shrouded in flowers like cenotaphs
Let us worship the living
The visionaries the revolutionaries the ill fitting
Let us clutch dreams as tightly as children's hands
Let us not appraise women's bodies as though they were curing meat strung from back yard
washing lines across the land
Let us read between the lines on our faces
Let us live quietly with our chosen families
Let us learn the language of lions
Let us listen
When the wind speaks
Let music not be anaesthetic but the heart's paratactic
Let poets be prophets
Let no person profit from another person's pain
Let us migrate
In great shoals of Arabic script across the skies and the seas
And finally

When they bury us

Let us remember we are seeds.

The Correct Spelling of My Name

You
who write revolutionary symphonies from beneath your single bed
who type masterpieces on back street Blackberries that will never be read
you who has never listened to a single word that you have ever said
who stopped listening to yourself years ago at the same time your elders did
And you whose eyes are sniper slits whose mouths are trenches
you whose friends are grey skinny birds gathered around broken park benches
pecking bread crumbs of ice
you whose hollow bones whistle with other songs
you who wears the right shoes but still never belongs
you the stiff tongue, you the mistimed
you the off beat, you the hurricane eyed
you pacifist soldiers.
you small girls folded into whispering corners
you quiet warriors. furious tomorrows.
you with scrubbed out lips and eyes that are afraid to close
you whose body will not fit into your prescribed clothes
irrespective of your size
survivors of gendercide
you counters of the abacus of stars
you shine eyes you exploding hearts
you whose moths are scars
you healing tongues you who understand two wrongs
will never make a writer
you freedom fighters you Saturday night survivors you long distance smilers
you who found your dream but could not spell it
who sat at the back of the class deciphering whiteboard hieroglyphics
you free-styling dyslexics
Council estate prophets
urban mystics
who publish poems on street corners from the printing press of your lips
whose eyes when cornered are a total eclipse
you who only learned at school that you were stupid.

that your name was Could Do Better
you who must work harder
you who retreats to the far corners of the cave of your hood
you who learned to beatbox by following the patterns of fist against skin
through a closed bedroom door
you are loved.
you with eyes of television static
you who practices your heartbeat on split lips
as soft and ripped as inner sleeve lyrics
you who stand in the shadows of the playground
muttering a hidden language
For whom the streets are your heritage
you who tattoo poetry against tenement buildings
you who is afraid to ask. Who never questioned.
For fear of not knowing. For fear of rejection
you who is the quiet eye of the classroom storm
you who will wait most of your life just to be born
you who cannot sit in the same room as yourself
who sits beneath the bed proof marking your body
you who was raised in captivity
who spits on the rusting links of your parents' economic slavery.
You rocking boy You flickering girl
who traces a map of an undiscovered world on your inner arm
how can they call it self-harm?
you who seek your identity at darkened parties in the clouded faces of strangers
who trace your ancestry with broken fingers
you beautiful believers. you courageous care leavers
you who were once lynched from a branch of your family tree
you whose anger is hereditary
whose smile is a flashing blade
whose weakness is brave
whose eyes are shallow graves
in which both your parents are buried
you who lost your family in the supermarket
at the check out

at the chill out
on the thin walk home
you who is a poem
you are afraid no one will read
believe

you are not a mark on a piece of paper
you are a prayer

Learn the correct spelling of your name

you who see a difficult sun when you close eyes
rise. You have found your tribe

Ollie O'Neill

Ollie O'Neill won the Poetry Society's national youth slam championships in 2013, and since then has performed across the UK at gigs and festivals, and has been featured in the Guardian in a piece about the rise of the female spoken word artist, as well as in the Huffington Post.   She is also published in the *Outspoken Anthology*, released in early 2015.

"Ollie O'Nell is a writer and performer of depth and passion who won the national youth slam SLAMbassadors UK in 2013. Her powerful and uncompromising poetry is both personal and political, and has the ability to elevate audiences to grinning tears. Since winning she has gone to develop a solo career performing for Outspoken, Chill Pill, Poetry Society, Apples and Snakes, Poets vs Emcees among many other. A voice that calls you home. This project allowed her to travel north and make new connections that will serve her well"

Joelle Taylor

On Being a Woman

Bring your body to the harvest before it is ripe
and watch them trip over their own tongues to be the ones that grow you.
While you are still bulb, still roots, still budding, still skin and bones and
Not yet fleshed, they will try their hardest,
To ensure it is their garden that you are planted in.

When you blossom:
Unevenly, clumsily, at odds with your own proportions,
Watch their flower beds turn to
Canine teeth. Watch your body become held breath.
Nobody will take you to the breakfast table now.

You are too loud,
You are too much,
You are all tempest temptress.
How dare you have the audacity to look like woman but smell like girl?
How dare you come here with your wide hips but your small hands,
Your red lips but your young tongue?

The thing with ripe fruit is that it is so easily pierced.
The thing with being soft is that everybody wants to touch you.
The thing about being a woman
Is that this was never your choice.

Advice to a Young Writer

1: If you leave a metaphor in your mouth too long it becomes sour.
The poems you write about men who tell you lies with their hands and with their tongues, the poems you write to un-write, are always the ones that will fly by themselves.
All words are permanent, and you can't take them back once you've given them to an audience.

2: If you only write to perform what you write will feel like plastic. It will chip your teeth. If you write of things you do not know you will speak them with an accent nobody else has but everybody recognizes. All lies sound the same, even if you sing them.

3: 140 Characters didn't kill the written word. I've received tweets far more important than any letters I've ever been sent. I've watched bonfires in in car parks I've cried in turn to sunsets of love I thought I'd never lose but know now I never had, know now I never want, know now I did nothing to deserve.

4: Not everybody can write. Even if their souls feel like they rhyme with yours, even if every-thing they let slip from their mouths pulls your tide in: Some people cannot hold a pen. It is as simple as that.

5: Some obituaries share the same words as wedding vows. Some words will always make you cry, no matter who says them and no matter where they are said.

6: It's dangerous to assign entire emotions to entire languages because when you inevitably end up feeling differently you will lose your mother tongue.

7: Only date a writer if you are prepared for every waking moment of your synchronised lives to be cemented in sentences, only if you are prepared for every inch of your skin to become paper, to become a canvas. Only if you are prepared to be set alight with absence, with separation. Only date a writer if you never want to read again. Only date a writer if you want to know how your mother intended your name to be said. Only date a writer if you want words to become nothing more than shallow grave stones for all the things you used to feel. Only date a writer if you want your language to become a scar on your tongue. A flesh wound. A reminder.

8: Never write poems for An Audience. There is no such thing. You will never know exactly how to make everybody's palms sweaty, you will never get everyone's hearts skipping every second beat to every second word, every mid rhyme. You will fail. When you start writing for An   Audience you stop writing for yourself.

9: Make sure that when you write your first love poem you know that your chest will always be large enough with pride to keep her home in. Make sure that when you write your first love poem you do it with your eyes closed. Make sure that when you write your first love poem you realise that most words are flames and when the time comes to bury them you will burn your hands.

10: Remember that people are not poetry. Do not let him bruise your skin with whiskey breath just because you love him and you think you could make something beautiful of it when the sun comes up. Sometimes there are no metaphors or similes. In the knuckle cracking adolescence that sets your heart on fire, sometimes it is just Mayfairs and Strongbow. Sometimes it is just smashed glass and razor blades. Sometimes it is just waiting rooms and days that feel as though they will never leave the ground. Sometimes it is just remembering that your hands are capable of holding as well as balling into fists. Sometimes it is learning that by your own hand your body may be barbed wire but there are people out there who will touch you like you are cotton. And sometimes that is enough. Just remember to write it down anyway.

Sunday

Sunday: I am spitting you into my bathroom sink. I am washing you out of my hair. I am shrugging you off. I am convincing nobody but myself. Rinse and repeat.

Monday: I am still picking pieces of your church from between my teeth. I am still drunk from your red wine lips. I am still full from your milk bottle skin. You are ambrosia and I have spent my whole life starving.

Tuesday: I cannot help but remember the ease with which you closed the space between our bodies. All sweat, all skin, all breath so as not to lose each other in the dark.

Wednesday: I am trying to find alternate spellings to your name. I am trying to find ways of writing poems that do not read like memoirs to the night you first taught me that my lips make perfect firewood. The night I learnt that my tongue will never be able to say anything even half as beautiful as the way that it danced up your spine to your neck.

Thursday: We haven't spoken in days and I am beginning to feel as though my mouth is home to a loaded gun. I would like to hear from you, but I am glad you do not call: I know inevitably I would end up saying something that would pull the trigger and then I would have no choice but to bite the bullet.

Friday: Our eyes are whispering to each other in the street light and I am tripping over my own laughter, begging to be let under your skin with wide eyes and flashed teeth. Your voice is slow, melodic, and we both dance along to questions we already know the answer to.

Saturday: Spring greets our pale, bed-warm bodies through the windows and I am finding it hard to tell where you end and I begin, all our angles blurred, softened by sleep. After the storm of the night before, I am teaching you about calm: Your mouth, our silence. On your forearm, I write 101 promises with my fingers tips: I will stop doing this. I will stop doing this. I will stop doing this.

Sunday: I am spitting you into my bathroom sink. I am washing you out of my hair. I am shrugging you off. I am convincing nobody but myself. Rinse and repeat

Harry Zevenbergen

Harry Zevenbergen poet, promoter and former official citypoet of The Hague. In his work political satire, sharp observation, a heartfelt tear and hilarious absurdism are alternated and juxtaposed. As a performer Harry has proved he can entertain all kinds of audiences. From a hardcorehouse gathering, to punkrockers to the poetryloving elite. In the past 19 years he has performed over 1200 times, including over 150 performances in Belgium, UK and Ireland. He has published four Dutch collections of poetry and one in English called *Save the last dance for me* (Witte Uitgeverij, 2010). Harry is involved in all sorts of socially focused projects and projects that promote talented poets from his hometown including the city wide Den Haag Schoolslam.

www.harryzevenbergen.nl
email@harryzevenbergen.nl
https://www.facebook.com/harry.zevenbergen

I'm not there

I control the chaos
up to a certain point
I tie one sentence to the other
with every word every letter
I'm a different person

I'm not who I was before
changed while I was asleep
after making love to you
I'm not the person who
capsized your life

when I woke up
I'd already forgiven your name

you're not the same
that entered my life
closed all the doors
threw away the key
you and me against the world

my past is willing
I remember what I need
and leave no traces

For You

the sky is clear
the thunder unexpected
a single lightflash
changes everything

cardrivers stop get out of their cars
to help a granny cross the road
cabdrivers take every single client
straight to their destination

in the shops everyone is talking
to strangers waiting for their turn
while emptying their shopping baskets
cause they do not need all that stuff

people buy poetrybooks instead of the Daily Sun
sit down and discuss the beauty of poetry
and the power of metaphores, rhyme and rhythm

peaceprotesters do get the message
all weapons are being collected
and reforged into more useful toys

the IMF and the Worldbank count all the money
and divide it equally amongst all people everywhere
policemen start talking in the first person

on the 8 o'clock news the queen sings
'Farewell to the crown' by Chumbawamba
and is joined on backing vocals by Charles,
Harry, William and the London Gospel Choir

she puts the Throne at speaker's corner Hyde Park
packs her bags and leaves the palacedoors wideopen
inviting the homeless people to take over the place

God takes his turn declaring:
'I do not exist nor do the others
and even if you still think We do
We're not worth killing for anyway'

this is how the world was meant to be
this is how my world looks
thanks to you......today and ever after

I'm not your clown anymore

we stand back against the wall
hell you can push no more
the wall will not give in
we will not give in

devolution power to the people
more power to some people you mean
Caring society means we can fix
what you fucked up and don't care for

you can push but you can hide no more
we know where your house lives

you lie and you steal
you start the wars you do not fight
you look like us
but real people burn in your friendly fire

in the trenches of a social economic war
you die in hospital in a home for the elderly
or by the overdose you took in desperation

curing useless people hurts the profits
devolution do it yourself 2015 style
a so-called caring society I don't care for
I don't care for the right of self-destruction

top down upside down
makes the world go round
free choice free speech
free lies and propaganda

you hide behind your fences
you hide behind invisible boarders
playing your neo-liberal game
to death and these are the rules

squeeze the working class, make them suffer
for a penny and laws to keep them down
lure the middle class to be the buffer
give them art and give them culture
and a payrise to keep them on your side

for you the upperclass
upper class no rules no tax
no blood on your hands
you don't break the law
you make the law
greed as raw as greed can be

you make the law make the law criminal
in your book you leave us to pick up
the small change
money unlike water
always goes to the highest point
unlike day to day problems

You ask why this poem isn't funny
I say you're not funny, never been funny
never will be funny only in a cockey
'potato in your throaty'
'blazery-rudy-private-schooly'
'let's hunt-the-foxy loony'
kind of way

I used to be innocent
my wit was sharp but the blade turned blunt
I do not want to make you laugh anymore
I do not want to be your clown

the day gets closer when
you'll be the lonely loony foxy
who's gonna get hurted hunted
now that's what I think is funny

Sanne Bartfai

"Sanne Bartfai is a young talented poet from the Hague. As a 15-year old she won The Hague Schoolslam 2014, the biggest slam for young poets in the Netherlands and the chance to be part of Intercity Flow. Her strong points are her imaginative writing and a natural strong but modest performance. She lets the words and images do the work.

"Intercity Flow involved two days of performance and writing. Two days amongst more experienced poets of all kinds really meant a lot. It made her take some giant steps, an experience that under 'normal' circumstances takes much more time. She has her own voice, with a lot of room there to broaden her horizons, try different approaches."

Harry Zevenbergen

Light

light is always looking for an exit
the world has to see his art
unexpected never seen a line so straight
never drawn before
turning the rainbow all red
we have seen the light
stop and go on

please let somebody freeze time
we will turn into ice
when we breathe
stop and go on
fly and run faster
till we burn and pass on

light will blind you
they who can see the light
will be dazzled
for the spirit that dies in here
moving to another piece of art
moving to the next colour

light is always last
darkness never shines
and without it
nobody will see the light
and if it shines no one
can see the light is burning
that light is crying
that light is last

Letter by letter

learning about life
a world full of words
words we don't understand
that will be known
if we turn the page
my head filled with new words
spreading the knowledge gained
learning for new adventures
a desire to blend into the story
eyes closed ready to embrace
ready for arms around me
arms unknown yet ready for
great stories, new secrets
eyes closed ready to hold
ready to tell what would scare you off
ready to be embraced if you could see me

The Limit of the Line

We draw the line at the horizon
Not knowing what keeps itself hidden
behind the coloured sky
The ability to speak of the desire to know
will be written in an extinct language.
Thinking that we understood what was meant
with words unspoken, we make mistakes.

Mistakes that keep us from trying again
beginning where it starts.
Walk the road again,
looking how to feel and understand.
Learn to write with a different alphabet
that by doing what's expected we'll fail.
Because each of us, we write our own story,
The sentences of another will not do.

Begging, we will speak in the
universal language of tears
hoping for understanding, a role
in someone else's life.
Then realising that we cannot write
with letters we were taught,
they limit us saying what we want.

Carmen Thompson

Carmen lives and writes in Saltburn-by-the-Sea. As the daughter of an Irish mother and Yorkshire fisherman her writing pulls together the magical, the practical and the visceral. She writes poetry and prose for page and performance. Her poetry has been described as 'crackling dangerously with inherited magic'. Carmen has been commissioned by and performed at London's Royal Festival Hall as well as Live Theatre Newcastle and other live venues. In 2012 she won New Writing North's Northern Promise Award for fiction. In 2015 Carmen became one of BBC Radio 3's Verb New Voices. Carmen has an MA in English Literature and Language from the University of St Andrews. Her poetry was previously featured in Ek Zuban's *Break-out Anthology*. She works on poetry, storytelling and creative writing projects with young people

More at: https://carmenellen2013.wordpress.com

Sister Circus

After your show, I don't sleep.
Dreamless I repeat,
All the different ways you sit
up and beg, your dinner
plate paws slack as mittens, all "Hey,
little sis – come to me."
I scream like a kid - sucker screams.
And then I do it all
over again. I put my head
on your cat-tongue, cheek
to pink papillae.
Then I sleep.
Pillow stuck to my cheek
with red iron drops.
I wash the sheets. Cells multiply.
Skin forgets. Days. Weeks.
You see me in the street.
Lights up. Repeat.

This time I followed you backstage,
watched you peel off your spots and drop
them in expensive oil. You crawled back
into your cage. You were cleaning
yourself ready to sleep when you
heard me. Then you made that
sound – yowl – like I had put a thorn
in your paw, like you were still on
show. That was enough for me.
"Come on", I said. Slamming
my palms against your cage.
I wanted to know – if you were still in there,
the real you behind the 'I love you' s,
the girl who cut me with one clean claw and

said you're mine or not at all.
I didn't have to shake so hard for you
to push out the meat of your jaw,
beating my heart between your teeth.
Yes, you're still in there, not even deep down.

Do you know the cage is open,
it has been all this time.
Don't you feel old? I do.
It's time to go. Go back to the Mangrove,
change your spots for clouds.
Or hang from your tree, wearing only leaf shadows
and I will forget it ever happened.
Go, before they turn you over,
on the dark road, to the canned hunt.

But here we are, me, you and the bars, "I'll let go
of them first if you come out here and finish me off",
I say, opening the red curtain of myself.
"Come out here and let me let you go".

Red Sky

It blooms on the Dune Slacks
by Adder's Tongue
Five fingered like sorrel,
red as hushed lips
They say it's juice will bring back the drowned.
It is called Red Sky.

The islanders keep to and are kept
alive by the colours they wear.
Green for a Wednesday.
Green for grass, land-skin,
furred and deep rooted
green to keep your children's feet from webbing.
Blue for web-foot.
Blue for bad luck.

Tyra watches with her bad luck eyes
the dawn sun spilling peach juice over cloud.
She watches a shadow in the water.
Her bread burns in the pan unwatched.
Her mother, Runa, chases out the smoke
and her naughty daughter,
out of the door into the bright morning.

It is the first day of Spring and
Tyra is given the green apron,
but her mother cannot cover her daughter's bad luck eyes.
Runa tells her daughter the way of it
Where to find the slender
shadows of the juicy fish.
And when to let the net go and lay still in the bottom of the boat,
keel to spine, and tip the bowl of her hips to the sky.
but Tyra is playing loop-finger
with baited lines and does not hear
when her mother tells her

do not look into the water.

The clouds part, cut-flesh red.
Runa wades out with Tyra kneeling
in the neat belly of the boat.
It is Tyra who pushes her mother away
A kiss goodbye is bad luck.

The open water is sun-stained,
rose gold with spray light.
Tyra arches over the side of the boat,
feeding the nets into the water.
The green apron, rough woven sea grass,
chafes her ribs as she bends.
She folds it square away in the bow.
She bends more easily now.
She looks at herself on the water –
Dark blue eyes and red lips.
Red as Red Sky. She smiles.

Deep below, where it is midnight always,
grey eyes watch back between the diamonds
of the drift net, he takes the gift of the ungiven smile.
He thrashes the wide iron muscle of his tail
moving up and up through all the colours of light.
His unbreathing mouth open,
closing on Tyra's red lips.
She can see the keel of the boat drift away
above her as he tips her hips to the sky.

Runa waits.
The boat comes in on the flow tide
with the oystercatchers,
empty but for the green apron.

The island people make a funeral, as they must.

Runa takes a handful of clay
from the ground to scatter
on the empty coffin where her
daughter does not lie, but she cannot let it go,
she puts the clay in her pocket.

Winter falls cutting through Autumn
with a crack of night ice.
Winter is strong and long fingered.
Runa makes crumbs from black bread.
The birds watch her with their tick tock eyes,
wound for the Spring that won't come.

Runa cannot sleep for the cold
and the twitching of her heart.

Runa takes the grave clay,
and mixes it with the juice of Red Sky.
She kneads it into a little doll,
and dresses her in a tiny green apron.
Then she leaves her gift at the tideline,
given to receive.

The near-night sky burns slap-cheek red,
A black curved shadow breaks the still water.
It grounds itself in the shallows.
Red hair swirling like dulse.

Bang bang bang.
Runa opens the door.
Mother and daughter embrace.
Runa's hands squeeze and snatch
Cheeks and hair, hands and feet.
Feeling for the life beat drumwise
of her lost child now come home.

But her own dear lost girl grins like an otter.

Her teeth chitter chatter over mackerel bones.
Silver scales stick to the pail where she bathes and
Grey gills flutter at the daughter's neck.
The girl's bad luck eyes do not see Spring turn back for her.

Spring. Eggs swell. Nests are raided.
Adders fill their bellies with baby mice.
Nets are made.
Tyra's belly swells.

Runa listens. Hears the thunder of the ocean
in the drum between her daughter's hips.

Summer. Berries droop.
Rabbits flatten green grass into dune paths.
Kestrels break their still and stoop.
Tyra's belly stirs.

Runa named Tyra for thunder.
They fight. The sand martins practise sleeping on the wing.
A birch leaf begins to burn from green to copper.
Tyra's skirts are bloody.

Autumn. Gathering time.
It is late for samphire but Runa gathers
its green flashes from between the rocks.
There in the heron pool, red dulse, red laver,
red hair and tiny green apron.
The gift given to take back.
Teep teep, Runa sends the curlews up
with her falling down steeped skirts.
To get home before the sun comes down.
Home. The sand martins are gone.
Home. Tyra is gone. The curlews teep teep.
No. It is another sound.
A blue baby stirs. Teep teep.
His name is winter.

Lauren Dye

Language has always fascinated Lauren Dye, so becoming a writer was inevitable. With an undergraduate degree in English Studies with Creative Writing, and an MA in Creative Writing from Teesside University, Lauren has discovered ways to make language bend and sing, forming emotional connections and truths within her poetry. She has worked on the organisation and promotion of live poetry projects on Teesside including Smokestack Readings and T– Junction international festival.

"What immediately struck me about Lauren's work was her ability to create a controlled and restrained form, but within this she sets fuses that blow spectacularly. This selection shows her range and skill and how she balances formal restraint with emotional integrity. 'Formation' playfully uses the sonnet form to constrain dark ideas and sharp observations. 'Playground' is a visceral, honest and playful unpacking of the roles a mother must play. 'Dear Death' is a slow building whirling dervish of a poem about little and big deaths. I hope you enjoy these works."

Carmen Thompson

Formation

His name was Ordinary, the colour
of hibernation or fallen ant hills.
He was shrugged off like dandruff spots on her
shoulder, stored in a cabinet of pills.

Behind him through white wisps of hair I see
seven birds in V formation pedal
patterns in the sky, pick their toothpick tree
twigs to land on, piercing flesh petal

blossoms with talons shaped like shattered glass.
The charge rang out, it shouted static, set
the birds searching sharp gazed through shredded grass.
Caught sight of a pricked ear, twitching wet

nose that knows the ants have left their mud mound
and thinks too slow, *quick, quick, get underground.*

Dear Death,

I'm honoured that you grant me so much of your time
I see the desire in your eye in every reflection
your face gazing at me from the pattern in the curtains
Even when I smooth it out you move along
            and ask me where I keep the knives

I hear you laughing in the leaves outside
            while I lay in bed
Your dancing casts cat shadows around the eaves
I struggle to breathe when you press the pillow over my mouth
            telling me to go to sleep

With that jolt I wake and you have gone to put the kettle on

You join me on a flight
I don't know where we're going but we are high
            and the plane has no walls
You take my hand and we jump as the cold air plants kisses
            on our cheeks
I can see inside skyscraper windows
skirts tucked into knickers wagging toilet paper tails and it excites me

My favourite time with you is the head on collision
            I see every time I blink
I hold the accelerator down instead of trying to brake
You turn the music up so we can listen to the crowds cheering

            and suddenly the roads are empty

I pull into a layby and it feels like we've been fucking for years.

But Death, let me ask you
If I get caught in the clothes horse as I collect the laundry
and it collapses around me
        or if the wire from the hoover grabs hold of my throat
            and sucks my air into its own lungs,
who would find me, like that, lying dead on the floor?

Playground

I desire
to shed my skin
peel it from my overworked muscles
discard it in the playground
for others to play with
play on
play in
While I sit
on the parents' bench
to watch
pushing a new-born
back and forth
back and forth
as it cries
and makes
my bones produce wings

To take us
up over the fires of hell
that sparkle
like candles on a birthday cake
but soon go out
and the guests all leave
and only
my birthday suit remains
and I button it up
adjust it for comfort
tuck the kids in
wish them sweet dreams

Kayo Chingonyi

Kayo Chingonyi is a London based poet, lyricist, and DJ. He is the author of a book of poems, *Some Bright Elegance* (Salt Publishing, 2012), and features on Darkstorm's *Mind Like Water* album (Bad Taste, 2013). Kayo is currently working on a new book and a collaborative EP with Rapsz Katai. He has been awarded the Geoffrey Dearmer Prize and shortlisted for the inaugural Brunel University African Poetry Prize.

As a creative writing tutor Kayo has devised and delivered workshops for The National Theatre, London School of Economics, Royal Shakespeare Company, YMCA, Poetry Society, English Pen, Half Moon Young People's Theatre, Pop Up CIC and Apples & Snakes as well countless universities, schools, youth centres and writer's groups across the UK and internationally.

https://kchingonyi.wordpress.com/bio/

The Colour of James Brown's Scream

I have known you by many names
but today, you are Larry Levan,
your hand on the platter, in the smoky
room of a Garage regular's memory.
You are keeping When Dove's Cry
in time, as you swing your hips,
and sweat drips from your hair
the colour of James Brown's scream.
King of King Street, we are still moving
to the same sound, though some
of us don't know it is your grave
we dance on, cutting shapes,
machismo lost to the beat
— every road man is a sweetboy
if the DJ plays Heartbroken
at just the right time for these jaded feet.
Teach us to shape-shift, O Legba,
you must know I'd know your customary
shuffle, that phantom limp, anywhere;
that I see your hand in the motion
of a couple, middle of the floor,
sliding quick and slick as a skin- fade
by the hand of a Puerto Rican clipper-man
who wields a cutthroat like a paintbrush.
Let us become like them, a moving ode
to sweat, ordering beer in a corporeal
language from a barman who replies
by sweeping his arms in an arc,
Willy Ninja style, to fix a drink our lips
will yearn for, a taste we've been
trying to recreate ever since.

Bridlington, Alabama

After 'Bigger Trees Near Warter', David Hockney

What does it augur that a painting of trees
in Yorkshire becomes a copse of poplars
buttressing a plantation in my mind's eye?
That dirt road stretches to the length of legend,
is wide as the river of an old folktale: *they waded*
neck deep in the water, carried those too small or frail.
Those distant buses must be Greyhounds
bound for Baton Rouge with *Coloured Folks*
on board sat in the wrong section, prepared
for beatings with batons in overheating,
windowless, cells. Even in the Saturday-quiet
of your home town where no lynch-mob waits,
lest my arm round your waist seems *reckless*. The eyes
on this high street wander to your hand in mine,
recalling a time when my ilk didn't mix with yours.
You're new to this scrutiny. I rue the day you wake
to find it a commonplace, when you can't help seeing
more than a picture of trees whose fruit is only fruit.

This poem contains gull song

though not song, as such, so much
as guttural injunction; such music
we forgot how to understand, since
it lacks that, carefully planned, sweetness
sounding, instead, of black-shod
clockers-on, the splash and clack
of shop fronts, cabbies sparking
tabs in the cold of a windswept rank
flanked by one of Monkchester's
lesser monuments; a sentry stopped
in his bronze tracks, steps echoing
the strains of an old tune hidden
in the genes of a new one—a left-behind
accent fizzing at the back of my tongue.

Shoshana Anderson

Shoshana Anderson is a poet originally from New York City, currently living in England. She has taken part in the Barbican Young Poets programme since 2010 and has been a member of the collective Burn After Reading, run by Jacob Sam-La Rose, since its inception in 2012. She can be found regularly performing at poetry events in and around London.

"Shoshana Anderson is attuned to the rhythms of speech. In her work we find the stops and starts of conversation but with an added focus on the significant details that lift a poem from simple anecdote to something richer; a balance between what Borges would call 'telling the tale' and, through playing with the sounds of words, making the poem itself an event. I first came across Shoshana's work when I was teaching on the Barbican Young Poets programme. I was struck by the rhetorical shape of her poems, how each one has a sense of occasion so that, though the poems examine everyday experiences, they always feel scrupulously crafted. "

Kayo Chingonyi

moving

in an airplane over the ocean somewhere between here and there, turbulence probably, that's how these things go, two glass christmas ornaments rock into each other. *you know how glass breaks.*

against itself in a cardboard tube, bought when your sister was born, hung six years later in the room you shared, paint gives way to friction. flaking off in quiet chips. like band-aids rubbing off in your sleep. you wanted it for the living room. *you know the way sun makes white into gold.* a simple thing, rolled up into something so small. we should have left it in its frame.
carried into a truck by a man in a light blue shirt made deep with sweat, a few dollar coins trickle out of a hole in the box. *you know the way metal rings when it hits the ground.* in your living room it would have been a racket but the engine is idling and it's one of a thousand boxes and they've rolled away now anyhow. three dollar coins from the year you were five and started losing baby teeth. you swallowed one by accident during breakfast. wrote a letter to the tooth fairy apologising that you couldn't give her exactly what it was she wanted. stuffed it under the pillow and touched the tips of your fingers to it while falling asleep. there was a dollar there the next morning, round like the sea, hard like the earth. maybe there was a letter. you don't remember but the coin was warm and the same size as everything you touched that day.

Hollowing

the ribcage is taking itself apart and lacing itself together.
over and under, over and under,
like the runner your grandmother sent for christmas.
a tight weave. not even the tips of
your fingers will fit between
the slats of your chest anymore.
good.

breathe it out and seal it up.
fill your mouth with rocks.
never let anything form.

a vacuum is infinite, isn't it?
big like the beginning and the end.
you are making something of the pressure
in your chest. it's always pushing. there
must be a use for it, that in and out echoing
chamber.

all the people are gone and grand central is still alive.

Tempering

you're exiting the atmosphere
too fast
no one is pushing you anymore
you don't know where you got so much energy

all this hurtling headlong into the sun
you're beginning to sweat
in your sleep
strip the bed
wash the sheets

shower
thoroughly
when you were thirteen
you let another girl
cover your forearm
in spray-on deodorant
then set fire to you
for fun
took all the hair off your skin
layers of dirt you didn't even know existed
dead things

long-standing structures
long since condemned
heat
and then quiet
you want to be that clean again

Dizzylez

Live performer and traveller from Avignon in the South of France,
Dizzylez is the creator of the 'Slam n Jam' nights (spoken-word open mics),
and has hosted them regularly since 2007. He was the Winner of the
'European poetry slam days' competition (Berlin, 2009). He is the author
and co-composer of two albums *Un, deux* (2011), *Aux anges* (2014).
He has toured extensively in Finland and Estonia, and taken part in
translation workshops as part of Runoviikko there.

http://www.dizzylez.com/

Slamming

Slamming is like trying, wishing to make the words sound well, create some fun

Slamming is like shouting bright-shiny verses up to the sun

Slamming is like feeling you will fly, become a sky citizen

Soaring to the Moon, travelling smiles

Dreaming with ears open wide

Slamming is like giving, giving some pleasure to the clouds

Singing so loud

Slamming is like being so proud

Feeling the strength of a super-wonder

Being the GrandMasterFlash of lightning, creating thunder, fighting against hunger

Slamming is like sharing rhymes and powers, making your thoughts dance,

Slamming is like feeling so fresh, feeling so free

Feeling your flesh alive

Free
Extract

We are free to believe in ourselves, rather than in God
We are free to believe in our dreams, rather than in the ones sold to us.
Despite the obscene real estate prices, we are free to have one or
several secret gardens
We are free to be our own architects
We are free to fit up our own inner spiritual space
We are free to believe in words rather than in facts
We are free to believe in fairy tales, in fact
We are free to believe in the therapeutic and magical powers of music
We are free not to be someone else's slave...or worse, our own slave.
We are free to help, encourage or congratulate
We are free to send flowers without Interflora
If we like it, we are free to stay underground
If we like it, we are free to get high on the ground
Deeply non-violent, we dig the regular (and sometimes violent)
practice of verbal sparring, at home or on stage. And anyways, don't
bullshit me cause my Uzi weighs a TONGUE.
Man or woman, we are free not to speak the same language.
We enjoy jazz, linguistics, gender and dialect mixes...and some people
feel free to call us International swingers...why is that ?
We are free to speak with our hands and bodies...yeah, let's forget our mouths
Sometimes, it makes a HOLE difference...
We are free to be rich, my tailors.
We are free to be actors, rappers, slammers, story or
tale-tellers...or simply entertainers...
(as long as it feels good and as long as we share...)
We are free to think new, to invent, especially if it's useless.
We are free to be lost in our thoughts...
Yeah, flying to the Moon is actually cheaper than you may think
We are free to go higher and higher...without stepping on anyone else's head
We are free to seek fame, it doesn't necessarily make us politicians
We are free to love life, noise, joy, twists, shouts..............hihaaaaaaaaaaaah !
And we are free to love the sound of SILENCE...infinitely...and more
than anything else.

A Trip to Italic

Well beyond all maps
There's a land where the views have changed
Where the streets are leaning
No royalty, nobody to bow to
Only honest folk, only worthy folk
And when expressing joy they do a hopping dance

In this leaning land, few staircases: too dangerous !
Rippling footpaths, winding here and there,
With the wiff of fresh mint from their borders
Paths where one gets lost, where one loves to get lost, where one loves to stretch out,
Where thoughts meander...
Pleasure is the rule, time matters little

Far from all maps
It is a country where all is in good taste, everything appetising
You enter in on tiptoe, for here...all is heard

The calm of the moonlight, the wind in the dunes
A faint rustling
Here all is sensed, everything is felt
A bouquet, a petal brushing past, lightly touching
It is here that we hear the flowers gently opening
It is in this land we love to get lost
Where we dream for hours standing in the desert
There where one can listen to the light
See the night in colour without the fear of looking soppy
In that beautiful land, stripped of all barriers, a peaceful happiness prevails
Tinged with a soft stink:

Toddlers in taffeta, toads totally tipsy, tipple their tequila
Titillating teetotallers tease a telepathic tortoise with twisted toothpicks
Teeny-weeny triplets trip over termites trying to trap a tiger

Well beyond maps
There's a land where words celebrate
Where people, without hang-ups, have a circumflex accent
In this evergreen land, where all is in bud, where anything can be born
Innumerable windows, endless shorelines, beaches stretching out of sight, pages of fine sand
In this ineffable abode, the men are all handsome hulks, the women all nymphs
They woo at a glimpse, they embrace, and set themselves on fire under the big hoax trees
One comes across lizards, an angry young runner bean
Coloured crayfish, fabulous syllables, green teeth cicadas
Hand storms, fabulous syllables
Symbols as cymbals, verbose bursts of verbs

Far from all maps
One sets off, a smile on one's lips, to flush out thousands of nuggets
Everything glistens, everything sizzles, everything crackles, everything flutters
Far from all maps
One topples; leaning intoxicated over a book

Mostach

Mostach is a composer and performer with UZBK. This group unites the work of two composers drawing inspiration not only from hip hop and slam, but also from reggae and World Music. The group has been working together in this way for five years now. They favour acoustic sessions accompanied by musicians and have managed to find a certain balance in their work thanks to the presence of a guitarist, a violinist and a beatboxer. Mostach lives in Avignon.

"Mostach has a really deep voice, writes clever lyrics and gives a great swing and musicality to each one of his pieces. He is one of the two emcees of UZBK, an interesting and unusual band that plays a live kind of hip-hop with a beat-boxer and a violinist. He is fast and open-minded; he loved meeting poets from other cultures and countries and this will further influence his work."

Dizzylez

Traduction

Harm another, through thoughts made actions
because you think too fast, measure then mangle -
mail the pulp to commercial street; that's what happens
when the gobshites, like trade winds, start blowing,
oh the mother of transcription!
Carrying the pride and imprisonments of the past
she tenders her reflections for more compassion
so she can digest legible messages
despite broken melodies and social distortion.
It's no joke!
The grind of analogical embellishments and linguistic deboning
with the symbolic, simple like mic (microphone)
without strife (without a fuss)
without surfing on the waves of the vagaries of mood
it's the crest for the grumbling surfer
with a frustrated, fixed plan: he is all
blonde locks and tan, he breaks into a smile,
an impression of life without suffering
and then

PROFITS FOR ALL!
LESS INCOHERENT FRAMEWORKS!
MORE BLUE BURNING FLAMES
LIKE ABUNDANT RIVERS!

PROFITS FOR ALL!
LESS INCOHERENT FRAMEWORKS!
MORE BLUE BURNING FLAMES
LIKE ABUNDANT RIVERS!

Ser-vile Civilians

Only really free outside his body
the container encloses the contents
clearly drunk on the proof of gold he does not own
the covenant buries the conventional
primarily because manners are not just for mealtimes
and the rogues are rancid, transforming reality
preaching the dream, only presenting the packaging;
an outpouring of white lies, a cupboard of cash,
sincerely as possible, but under the skin these targets
are tainted by undeclared interests
hungry for negative stereotypes.
The peripheries bear the heaviest load
and it's a buzz
rattling
my body to the bone
I strip it bare, I worry it,
for only unadorned can it wear the truth-
just a little sensitivity in this world of well-groomed brutes.
I watch with spider eyes from my star-stilled web
the roofs provide no shelter
the dogs remain unstirred
they only woof or play dead at the bark
of a cunning kid, you win
by keeping your distance,
you fall again and again for the best of these bitches
and you don't give a damn about arguing the toss
to a society with such a vile soul
and you are bound to see it
in the calming prism of the dawn
so that hatred of the other doesn't emerge
victorious, civil obedience to a
statue of the state -
a blacked-out cock-up during a piss-up

that ended up set in stone
wasting away from head to toe
thinking of the burdens of yesterday;
men set at each other's throats without realising
then report back to this monument of many faces
that looks to divide the twilight into horrible expressions
without doubt or delay
once pride inspires the stone.

A Shake of the Head

All the sounds put together on the scene
I see the music more like a pregnancy
That shakes the brain-basket (head lost in word-play)
Check yourself out in your cliques vomiting your texts
It's you, it's me, but in the confusion
I'm surrounded by abundance
Happy to escape these closed circuits: sad and dull with shared baggage
You make a mutual vow with your soulmates –
A little more certain: no ass but assured
Sharper and stronger at Destiny's Door
My tongue, you hold no feast but that's the rub
Aye, that's the rub, I know my classics,
That's why I love music,
It's for that I hate the bollocks on the radio
For my ego. Egotism, for my thirst for life
Not mere curiosity I forgive myself
For not being the reflection of what I'd want to be
No, not for money, I don't want millions
Not the raging crowd, but I envy the violin
Which cries that they are fools of reason
That the good play
That the losers win
That some whisper
And the others feign
Plaintive suffering
And from that there is a surfeit

Jo Colley

Jo Colley is a writer, events organiser and digital learning designer who lives in Darlington. Jo has been described as "a thrilling, audacious poet, her language playful, exotic and rich, and she holds her nerve." (S.J. Litherland)

She has been published by Vane Women, Ek Zuban and Salt and her latest collection, *Bones of Birds* was published by Smokestack in March 2015. Her work has appeared in the *Black Light Engine Room*, *By Grand Central Station I Sat Down And Wept* (Red Squirrel Press), *Kumquat* and *Ink on Paper* (mudfog / mima).

She has worked as a poet and prose writer running creative writing sessions with people of all ages and backgrounds. She was reader in residence for both the Darlington and Durham Book Groups, in association with New Writing North, and curates poetry events such as Babel and Poetry Parlour in Darlington. She co-hosted Darlington's legendary Hydrogen Jukebox Cabaret. She has also won prizes for poetry films and for short stories and flash fiction.

Losing Weight

"You feel like one of Uncle Eric's rabbits," he says,
lifting her above his head. His hands almost meet
around her waist, make an hourglass to accommodate
a single grain of sand.

She pictures blurred bunny shapes, ribs showing
against drawn skin, eyes like watchful globes
as the old man pulls them from the hutch,
holds them up for examination.

Too thin for the pot, too weak
to make a run for it. Stillness is the only
option, as they wait for something,
maybe the wind, to change.

Bonnie Parker's Rabbit

Way down the road, Henry shot the traffic cop
for no reason. She was mad as hell. Held
the man's head on her lap, gave him the last
of her water. His life flashed before her eyes:
a rookie, spruced up for his first day on the job,
his mind on wedding day plans, now cancelled.

Later, Sonny Boy's soft mass takes the cop's place,
and her hands lose themselves in the familiar rhythm.
But it's no good. She feels like her neck is broke. Makes
Clyde stop the car and shoos the rabbit out into
the midnight fields. He glows ghost-like for a second
then takes off across the scrub, taking his chances
under a harvest moon.

Rowan

By the time we got to the last one,
she'd stopped crying. Her eyes,
brown, pitiful, were clouded now
like she was already dead.

None of us wanted it this way,
least of all Piotr, but the stones
require a woman's heart to settle.
Nothing else will do.

Her last breath, a small, sweet sigh,
like a bubble reaching the surface
of a dark pool. Enough to seal the pact,
to heal the cracks that might destroy.

The way the morning sun stole in
fingered the walls with a yellow light
casting a blessing on our gift. She slept
like a baby under a quilt. Safe.

Later, when spring came,
a thin green stick found its way out.
By the summer, a whole tree, branches
waving defiance, leaves muttering.

White flowers accused us,
drove us mad with the scent of tears.
Then the berries, blood red, profuse.
We found Piotr hanged.

Serena Rana-Rahman

Serena Rana-Rahman started writing poetry at the age of 14. A general love of literature led her to gain a First Class BA (Hons) degree in English Literature at Teesside University. During her time at university, Serena began to participate in creative writing activity and won a competition to become a member of the Intercity Flow programme. This is Serena's first publication. Serena performs often at The Electric Kool Aid Cabaret, and other local literary events.

"Serena knows about form. I have been impressed by her ability to work with this knowledge and to admit the unconscious. I also wanted her to understand the need to make a poem coherent – not necessarily easy to understand, but to express its own logic. My favourite of these poems is Goat Telepathy. It maintains its affectionate, instructive tone throughout, and has both humour and mystery. Intriguing and satisfying. As I was at the time writing rabbit themed poems, I feel like we had an unconscious influence on each other – part of the enjoyment of the mentoring process."

Jo Colley

The Tiger's Eye

My bare feet press against each grain of earth,
press and press until dust and mud forms lines and roads upon the sole.
With eyes to perceive
and lips to read
and teeth to tease
we shall feel the world with our fingers and claws
and through each marbled-apple eye,
like a globe or an egg yolk.
Even air has detail,
the silent emptiness passes through the ear
and we hear the sound of that familiar stillness
like the artist's brush dances against the page in swirls of grey.
Or perhaps the dreams that refuse to leave our lids for weeks and years,
without fading as we age.
I have watched blue ink sink into my skin and drawn a map leading to my heart.
There is detail in the red fruits that sit in the palm and burst into flames,
like the sky on a hazy October's night.
There is detail in a fistful of sand,
and the way it hurries to fill the lines of the hand,
like dripping candle wax
and the flickering flame,
as it rises - then burns
like the tiger's eye
There is detail in the moon
as it hangs in the sky like a freshwater pearl.
And pools of rain,
where water falls like tears to the thirsty earth.
The detail in your words that linger and lurch,
have left me sleepless and perturbed
like tempestuous wind.

There is a clock across the hall

Black, rusty, staring with tired eyes
for each hand is weighed down by dust,
collected as each minute passed,
pushing back the heavy seconds

A day has never passed when time did not follow us,
taunted us, slipped through our fingers
like sand or water we never can grasp;
like each breath, drawing closer the moments we dread
and further from the moments we have lost.
Like the tide, it washes our memories and discolours the mind.

When someone asked
Have you seen the time?
No I did not, for it passed too quickly before my eyes.
where did time go, when I was a child and slept so soundly in your arms
and felt the beating of your heart, like the ticking of a clock.

Let me hold your hand and trace the lines that have deepened.
Let our lives, like pages turn and turn and form the earth that time corrodes,
I remember the bicycle I owned when I was eight,
and when I rode, its wheels spun like the curves of a dark spiral clock.
I remember the curves of his dark eyelashes,
lest time should ever let me forget.

Everything must be measured in time,
but why live confined to the ticking's of a mechanical clock?
A heartless piece of cold metal
yet one we cannot seem to live without.
This I say, but tomorrow I know, its sound will chime
and to it, I will rise.

Goat Telepathy

Of the many people I have met,
None have mastered the mind of a goat as I have.
A goat is like an exam, a study in Goatness,
Although his mind will always be supreme.

First, let me expel the many goat myths you may have heard.
Yes, a goat will nibble everything, but carefully chooses what he digests.
Of course he will not eat a tin can, whoever believed this old wives' tale
But he may pull your hair, nibble fingers and yank coats, boots or trousers.
He will tug you like a rag doll, and explore your humanness like a new world.
He is the fussiest of eaters, and requires fresh vegetables, along with delicious fruit
It's true; they will not eat food that has touched the ground,
Unless of course it's chocolate.

A goat is not smelly, in fact, he is rather particular about his house and home.
He will clean the ground before he sits,
Or his brother may clean his fur lovingly like a mother.
Did you know a goat can tell time?
Like an alarm clock, bellowing near dinner time
And wondering why he cannot stay up till after midnight.
One thing that's certain, a goat has more character than three people put together.
Goats are like cats, they hate the rain – you try giving him an annual bath,
and just to make clear – no, I don't take him upstairs and put him in the bathtub.
And also, to clarify: if a goat is a boy, he *can't* give milk
Just in case you were going to ask.

Goats worship the sun,
Basking in its warmth like a cat.
Interesting fact: goats do not have top teeth,
Strange you may think, but it's like one big gum,
Just as well – thank God my mother's windowsills were spared.
Goats are exceptionally good climbers,

They can climb a tree like we walk up stairs
And will stay there all day, like the ornaments on a Christmas tree.
Trampolines are good for goats to climb, they make good seating too.
Imagine, a goat sitting on a trampoline.
And *both* male and female goats can have beards,
just like us really.

Goats rarely eat grass, so don't expect him to replace your lawnmower,
He'd much rather eat your shrubs.
Goats are so impatient, so I wouldn't even bother trying to train him
He is far too independent and of course, his own boss.
As I mentioned, goats do not eat *everything*
But I think it's fair to say, *"sorry sir, my goat really did eat my homework"*
They are not too keen on smarties, mini eggs or any form of shelled chocolate
 - remember, I did tell you they are fussy.

Apart from bleating,
when he *really* means business,
he can make a rumble-noise from his throat
the first time I heard it, I was 12 years old
And thought we had a Tyrannosaurus in the back garden.
It was just his way of telling me to get lost.
But now it's different as I've grown up,
He'll just swing his head and hit me in inappropriate places
- believe me, I'm putting that *politely*.

Goats do not like children. I think it's the screaming,
after all his hearing is super strong, just like his sight.
Did you know goats have a warning sneeze?
It's quite complex, but I think I've managed to figure it out.
If he sees a threat he delivers a sharp sneeze-like noise,
To warn his friend to be alert, and usually
Makes the human believe there's a murderer in the garden,
When it was probably just the neighbour's cat.
He does not like you to stroke his forehead,

His shoulder is a much safer bet.
But if all else fails, he'll come and place his backside in your face
To say, massage my legs, it's like having a back scratch.

A goat is like an inventor,
Always patenting ways to outwit the dizzy human,
When she is not looking -
Like a curious toddler's hand,
Delving into her pockets – opening the button
sliding the zip back,
emptying the contents with his teeth.
A goat knows the difference between play fighting and fighting.
Like a little lamb, he can choose to tap your leg ever-so-gently with his head,
Or like a lion, with fierce red dragon eyes,
Chase, charge and realise your first near-death experience.
Like a titan bull, his anger spreads like fire.
So I'd recommend carrying a water pistol.

But when a goat loves, he loves you like his own.
I should know,
For I have had the very hair on my head cleaned by one,
He licks my ears, cleans my neck
Falls asleep on my chest.
So even a dragon can be tamed,
And by the end of the day,
I am kissing his eye lids,
And when I look,
I can see the whole world,
Right there,
Swimming inside.

Jacob Sam La Rose

Jacob Sam-La Rose's poetry has been characterised as vivid, masterly and carefully structured. His most recent collection *Breaking Silence* (Bloodaxe) was shortlisted for both the Fenton Aldeburgh Award and the Forward Poetry Felix Dennis Award. He leads the Spoken Word Education Programme at Goldsmiths University and the Barbican Young Poets programme, and is widely recognised as an indefatigable facilitator, mentor and supporter of young and emerging poets. He travels and performs his own work nationally and internationally. He lives in London, England.

The Poem as an Ark

The poem has an appetite for everything, and wears its hunger well. The poem has evolved a taste for heroes, muted palettes, untidy endings. The poem knows the spirit of the season and exactly how its taste is different from the last. The poem carries a city in its belly, a living city — fierce light in every window, a geometry of streets as orderly as library shelving. The poem inks a label on its skin for everything ever held in its mouth. The poem is less concerned with memory than re-making. When sounded out, the poem unfolds its tongue as a blueprint for everything lost. Thinking of its swallowed treasures, the poem purses its lips.

Some Tentative Definitions: Red
After Kwame Dawes

As smell? Pure heat, and rising
from a heaving room, packed

wall-to-wall; and riding on each surge
and swell of bass and crackling rhythm.

Below: a curdling farrago
of perfume, stout and sweat.

Above: a bulb (a dangled blood moon) — sly
and brazen in the soft-edged dark.

On the Way Down

Above us, the universe sighs, doing the Heraclitean slide,
a tune whose chorus we sing by living. Clang clang.
— 'Lives of the Painters', Kevin Stein

We started soft.
No talents in amongst us.

    clang

There was a coach for a short time.
American. Ex-NBA. We learned
to hate him for man-handling the dream
into unforgiving light. Under his pin-point scowl
we were either good enough or not

    clang

the gulf between, a proving ground
of shuttle runs and 'suicides' that left us
open-mouthed like supplicants, and soon
we came to wonder what his damage was,
what injury or loss had brought him to us.

    clang

Still, we toughened up, sharpened against
each other; muscled up, to fill each gym's hot air
with something of ourselves. Each court
became a place to practise how
to put a question up and hustle

    clang

when the answer came down wrong;
how to survive each minor loss
and pick it up again. And on, and on,
the constant singing of the balls
became a hymn.

    clang

We learned the different names for want,
the math and physics of desire, faith.
And lost each fixture. No 'Hail Mary' came
to pass. Not one step closer to heaven. Coach,
darkening on the sidelines.

    clang

And soon enough, like most of us, I quit.
Went back to summer pick-up games
for different stakes, and found them pure.

Rachel Long

Rachel Long was shortlisted for Young Poet Laureate for London 2014. Her poems have been published in numerous anthologies and magazines, including *Homesickness & Exile* (Emma Press), *Magma* and *Synaesthesia*. She is a current poetry awardee on the Jerwood/Arvon Mentorship Scheme (2015-16). Rachel has facilitated poetry workshops in schools, libraries, and for organisations such as Apples & Snakes and Crisis at Christmas. She has curated events for Unheard Festival, Deptford Cinema and Tate Britain.

"There's much to admire in Rachel's work, and I mean work in the broadest sense, not just as comment on what's finally offered up as finished poems. Like many of the best of us, she's tenacious. Committed. And courageous. That's not to say invulnerable— she wears her vulnerabilities well, each time in service of the better poem. And that sense of service extends through the breadth of her work: a manifest appreciation of poetry as a practice that extends beyond the self. In all of this, I'm excited by both the poet she is and the poet she will become."

Jacob Sam La Rose

Sandwiches

Tiff's pressing me against school railings,
doing my eyeliner. This is how we meet proper.
I whisper in class, 'Your eyes.
Can you make mine like that?'
Like graphic novel knives.

Break-time:
Against make-up rules and railings – the diamonds
we chat with our fingers inside. We want
engagement rings this big, so big
we can see freedom on the other side.

Her weight against me is solid and soft, a bomb
before, then after, it goes off. A weight inclusive
of the glitter on her lids, the oil spill on her lips, the sandwiches
padding her bra. Yes, the sandwiches; unbuttered, no filling -
this is their purpose, not privilege.

See, the boys know the difference
between tissue and tit, a sock and a tit,
but not yet a tit and a slice of bread.
Tiff's so smart, my new eyes weep.

Sunny Side Up

Dad, you looked like a fried egg on your wedding day,
in your crisp shirt and yellow tie.
A yellow tie to your own wedding?
A yellow tie full stop.
I stole the photo from Mum's shell box -
the only thing grabbed from Nigeria. The only thing
she found herself still clutching at Dover.
Now it holds our passports, home
insurance docs, spare car keys. The jewellery
either lost or sold. I'm not sure
if Mum has kept this photo because she glances, still.
Or because, to her, you're just another
yellowing deed.

Patience of a Sports Watch

Dad brushes his teeth standing on one leg
to exercise balance. He reads
three minutes of 'A Walk To Freedom'.
Bleep-Bleep. Switches to The Guardian,
three more minutes – burpees up the stairs,
into a lukewarm shower. He even bleeps three drops of olive oil
into his palms, dabs *like he's afraid of it*,
Mum says, *this is knowing black people half his life,
his lot don't moisturise.* Bleep-Bleep. Combs his hair
til teeth grin in it. Bleep-Bleep. Collects a shopping list,
miss anything and you'll get no dinner at the bottom of it.
Packs files and pencil case - *Christ, have you ever heard
of a fifty year old with a pencil case?* - into his rucksack.
Bleep-Bleep. Late again. Shovels porridge from a bowl
balanced on car bonnet. Goes to the boot,
pulls out his cycle-to-work-scheme
- a work we've never seen. Bleep-bleep.
Mounts it. Waves to me with his screeching hand.
Mouths, 'Daddy loves Rachel.'
Ha. What sort of Social Worker can only voice their love in third person?
Bleep Bleep Bleep.

Claus Ankersen

Claus Ankersen, intergalactic traveller, has published 5 books of poetry in his native Denmark, where he is a leading voice in performance poetry. The author works bilingually in Danish and English and has done readings in 18 countries, while selected pieces have been translated into 11 different languages. Claus works cross-disciplinary; in 2009 he made a feature length documentary on Danish spoken word and in 2014 he received the Fencepole award for best public works, the 20x3 meter letter stelae installation 'Always'. Claus is also a Board-member of Finnish Runoviikko and is a member of Baltica Littera. This Autumn he will be published in the Ukraine and the UK.

https://www.youtube.com/watch?v=4VYXKHkXJKA

Imperial clothes

On the transition which never came and the failure
of the sheeple to be grasped by the rapture of twelve stringed
DNA promised but never delivered
we slither into forgetfulness to the drums
of the techno-industrial demon now dressed in green
windpowerplants a million miles high
covering every inch of available silence
now water-torture with wings acoustic
poisoning of the elves and the tears
the river of man is turning in on itself
running down the whole as one. Now it will never be tomorrow
and tomorrow will never be now
we are stupefied to find they are still ticking
the clocks being us with nowhere to go
but round and round a juniper bush, an antenna or a golden calf and
down into the sugar-mines and back up to the waiting screens chasing forever
the now we can almost remember
but never grasp that the said transition came – redemption was here
as absolute now while we were all busy looking the other way

SALTBURN-BY-THE-SEA, MATE*

Saltburn-by-the-Sea, mate
the giant cows on the cliff, mate
two stories high, mate, mirrored
mooing from bottomless pint glasses, all them grasses
It's the Olde Trip town, mate
Danish Bacon town, mate
It's actually quite the expert
in holding its breath
while the Sea sings on the shore
and the lone furnace relentlessly practises sundance
  under a Corto Maltesian twin moon
  under it's exquisite skin
of white bricks, and labour-blood
run hot on the inside
of centennials circling in a hidden backroom
playing bluegrass for the 25th year, just
because it is Tuesday
we finish off with a curry and stand
with one leg in Madras and dream
of dragons gliding out of the mist
on the shores
of Saltburn-by-the-Sea.

On my second morning
in the church called dining room
my thoughts are still ghost-ridden
I can feel them benched around me at the table
they must have followed
me down the stairs. I guess
they are still hungry for more. In my mind
I offer them fatty scraps
from both slices of bacon, now
settling in my stomach, bobbing on waves

of acid and thin, black filter coffee
half a baked tomato
mushrooms and a longish brown sausage.
This will be another good day
The tomato was nice and juicy, high blue skies
as yesterday
I am alone with my thoughts
and the ghosts
otherworldly as per intention of the builder
son of a Quaker industrialist, who gestated this house
as sanatorium for the workers
of that dark revolution, foresight really,
an offer of amends
for propelling the planet too fast, back
into the future. There is
a peculiar squeaking sound
behind the rumbling of the refrigerators
an old rusty swing in some
long forgotten garden of an abandoned house.
The ghosts must be cold, I can hear teeth chattering
like bones rattling
over their thick woollen mould: suits once.
An old couple enters, we greet each other
and I wonder if they too
have followed me down the stairs.
The ginger ghost man orders porridge
and the waitress with the stingy grey eyes serves it
a second later: one porridge, it is good
for your ghostly cholesterol, ginger-ghost smiles
I don't have any cholesterol, the waitress skeleton
replies. The ghost-wife eats toast
while a famished young man-ghost dressed
in the same mint-green as the church walls
routinely serves himself
a full English breakfast.

A young blue waitress glides by my table
in a whisper:
Well, are you inspired?
Most definitely I am, looking up at the sunlight playing
silent organ on the mosaic panes of dining room-church
windows
It is the best town, she concludes. I agree
The best town is where you live
Saltburn-by-the-Sea, mate.

*Dedicated to Andy Willoughby, Bob Beagrie and the people of Saltburn-by-the-Sea

I am farmer, and nomad is my name
(a poem on 'The Ethos of Place' and poetic nomadicity)

There are too few nomads in the world. Along the way
too many farmers. But I like farmers.
There is one thing you've got to know about farmers. Farmers are friendly*.
And I don't mean people working with agriculture
although these people can be friendly too.
Farmers are: people who stay in the same place for most of their lives.
90% of the earths population, they say, people who stay, they say at the same place,
forever accumulating goods and acquisitions. Hunting for savings in the supermarkets
instead of hunting animals in the forest. Gathering Chinese electronics
instead of gathering berries and roots.
These kind of farmers. Consumer farmers.
They are friendly. Especially if you take interest in their land
since they seem bound to their locality, in a sense
they become land
they never leave until they are buried underneath it. When we visit, us nomads
they meet with interest and curiosity, us
wayfarers being
exotic things from outer space, just passing through, funny little interludes
welcomed entertainment. A boat
with bananas, a band of gypsies, sailors
from strange and unknown shores;
poets, snake-charmers, funny men.

The farmers are friendly
especially when praised and commended
for their choices and accomplishments
for their skills at cutting coupons and corners. This poem
is turning into a walk in the fields somehow, an academic discussion
so let's talk about something really interesting, let's talk me
my frontal lobes were not properly developed, see
due to premature birth

my initiation into nomad-hood, shamanically speaking
was two months in an incubator, a glass cage, a transparent coffin
making me forever walk transcendent
in perpetual zen and empty becoming
these twin black holes, voids,
these gates
behind my forehead
star magnets making me fly. But that is a story for another night,
how nomads and poets always long
for a belonging they can not embrace and rarely fathom. But now let's talk about farmers.
Farmers are nice.
But there are still too few nomads in the world.

*Addendum: Only farmers can criticize farmers.
Farmers might say
"Who are you to teach us about our ways, lecture us on tradition? What WHAT
do you know about waking up and going to bed at the same time
in the same place
with the same people
in the same way, every day? What do you know
about fighting the same windmills,
about always being measured against your neighbor? What
do you know about solitude and stony hearts full of dirt and pebbles?
What do you know of Sisyphus?
You
are free. You are a bird. And tomorrow you will sit at another farmer's table
in another town. On another planet".

The nomad might respond
"Oh, don't tell me about loneliness. You have everything.
A wife keeping your bed warm at night, children
who will carry on in your image. You are immortal
even though you never move. Immortal. You are everywhere
You go everywhere, just by sitting on the same bench
by the roadside

you make the world come to you, see
the grass is always greener
for farmers and nomads alike.

Farmers are nice. Did I tell you that
one night in Bangalore, after a festival, left to my own whorish wordly dances
I took an auto to Koshy's, had vegetable curry, a paratha, fried fish and beer
and among all the other nomads and waiters dressed in white
I faced my Karma Bhoomi:
I am a wandering wordsmith
as fleeting as the wind.

I am farmer, and nomad is my name
I am nomad, and farmer is my name
always hunting for shadows and words
in invisible ink
written across from my table
by lovers and strangers alike. Putting them into my cauldron
and stirring with ink on a page (to be continued...)

Koshy's, St. Marks Road, Bangalore, February 11th 2015.

Maja Petrea Fox

Maja Petrae Fox appears regularly as a poet and poetry and music host performing at venues like The Royal Danish Theatre, Copenhagen Main Library, and various jazz clubs, cultural outlets and pubs. Publications:-roof tiles *As Tangents* (2013, self published)- *OPEN* (2015, Copenhagen storytellers). She blogs at http://majapetreafox.blogspot.co.uk/

"If there is such a thing as a modern day 21st century female beat poet, Maja Petrea Fox is pretty close to being it. She is young, a poet in the making and even though she has just published her first collection she is quickly building a reputation and fan-base with her charismatic stage presence, professional performance and – most importantly – her observant, sensitive and brutally funny-honest poems. I am so glad that Maja accepted my invitation to join The Intercity Flow project."

Claus Ankersen

Untitled

I prefer black hats, crows 'n' cats
in the night-time
where the moon moans
and we can dance around
in just bare bones
I prefer the grief of a fallen leaf
floating fanatically feminine
with only the sweltering dirty ground
as its final destination
I prefer bending street lamps behind
the curtain of tomorrow
twisting themselves in the arms
with a question of
melancholy gentleness
Can we play, Miss?

With my feet in the sky
and my head on the ground
give me black feather-filled wings to fly
between the petrol monsters
with only one sound
of the circus conquest of this world
where clowns are certainly clowns
and you do what you were told
wandering around without names
hoping for some kind of blue-rescue
delusionary and ridiculous
for a further spoon of midnight
but the bridge's on fire
home can't be found anymore
everything that I admire.

Cancer City Container

Shambling - and rambling existences by an eternal goal-rushing
down the street by dragging themselves
Like - greengrocers in the morning again, and forever sets
fruits into the street patently-strange and loving in long straight rows
As - the people march in the subway like dead birds on the way to work
shitting themselves on bicycles when they encounter a foreign object on the asphalt
So - pleasantwarm during the barefoot summer
despite pads soles get pink red nicks and hurt
As - armpits-of-junkies in streets make themselves happy
by finding a funky fix in the street behind the main course
Like - a big, powerful man with a cigar in the night
when I'm approaching with holes in my shoes in the dark
only lit up by neon lights distanced on the roofs
while the voices hum from the bars and out on the sidewalk
with smoke and tales of tomorow
lists out through the door of sorrow
in a long and straight bore-enticing
As - the yellowclear&brown liquids' prices change
from house to house, from door to door all over the city
Like - a great snorting and coughing steel machine
which eats several hundred servings of soul and coal every day
As - the day of yesterday equals in tow to the next
sun and moon over the buildings and chimneys
Who - plays the slow jazz dancing
beyond the stone bridge and through railways
As - the entire city's many corded veins
head on the window among teenagers in love
and people with tragedies on their clothes - in the train
Quietly - bobbing my body back to childhood
to the heart's rhythm - the city's rhythm in my heart
As - unending concerts at venues
autographs in dressing rooms with coke in

and my own stage fright
There - only is nonexistent in the middle of cobblestones
on an equal footing with the buildings and crows
As - the only thing you can be absolutely sure about
are tomorrow and the day after
As - the post-apocalyptic soldiers and hangovers
As – we were living right now, now now
in this, Cancer City Container, of love.

Beat

Beat is one man's mattress in the corner of the room

Beat is the beetles crawling out of the cracks in the old apartments, when not fussy

Beat is beautiful - Beat is the day today - Beat is what you want

Beat is to paint the town outside the marked edges

Beat is good style galore

Beat is laughing at the moon with yellow teeth, not knowing what tomorrow brings

Beat is the roaring saxophone at La Fontaine, on Fridays, Saturdays, Sundays, Mondays, Tuesdays, Wednesdays and Thursdays

Beat is when you sit at the front of the cargo bike and swing your legs over the edge, with cardboard wine in your hand

Beat is my bare breasts in the middle of the morning coffee

Beat is the foreign arm around you in bed Sunday morning

Beat are brown bars with the boys

Beat is the block, on luck and endless time

Beat is the empty pockets of your jacket

Beat is a bulkhead in your packet of cigarettes

Beat is downtown without being Down In The Gutter

Beat is NOW NOW NOW and half a box of beer dragged by several hands

Beat is waking up Tuesday morning and being higher than the man above and running out to greet yesterday in the toilet bowl

Beat is when everything must go, everything must go, everything must go

Beat the words burned into the skin with ink

Beat is when you decide to become healthier and stop smoking for twenty minutes, and then smoke 1 2 3 4 cigarettes after the other, to once again to fill your nicotine deposits

Beat is a french kiss so wet that the Atlantic subsides in deep cry

Beat is the mainstreet without panties

Beat lives on the sixth floor and Beat has a bad noise all night and all the way to the day after - Beat is Kerouac, Ginsberg & Uncle Danny met Burroughs in 1983

Beat is Bukowski grinning with a chicken in his hand

Beat is Waits, Coltrane and Gillispie Moanin' after Mingus – Beat is the rest and indifference

Beat is hip and newborn, every morning

Beat is when I go through the city on a cloudy day with sunglasses loaded

Beat is throwing bottles for pleasure - Beat can not be bought today - Beat is black coffee and black hats - Beat cigarettes on bricks - Beat wins the election every year - Beat is the wind in your spring - Beat is the excuse to get your mascara stuck in your hair - Beat is the dirty sheets and to visit your parents with the hope of dollars

Beat is dripping from the sky of neon and multicolored advertising - Beat is scratchcards' profit on a dollar, while you feel like a winner - Beat plays billiards and cheats while no one is looking - Beat snaps to more than jazz tones - Beat is far back from nowhere - Beat is to dig the misted windows on facades and half flat and greasy pint glasses

Beat is the bass and playing dice on who is giving an order

Beat is the white chopper in back rooms before closing occurs

Beat is open 24/7 and has more items than 7-Eleven

Beat takes the norm and shits on it

Beat is new, vintage, and effectively against stains of all that does not saturate

Beat gives you a constant erection

Beat is when you take to the city without money and behave as if you own a million

Beat is madness tumbling out of the honed edges

Beat is to throw sticks on street corners - Beat has no plans - Beat is the town, the place where everything IS bigger - Beat is people who are crazy, tender and up and running - Beat is just a little more - Beat is when life calls - Beat is to be obsessed by the writing moments - Beat is the words that live - Beat is the rummage shop, in the corner of Ikea.

Acknowledgements

We would like to thank Valerie Harkness, Dreg, Ghazala Bashir and Anton Flint for assistance with the translation of some of these texts, Jill Morgan, Michael Lavery, Chris Thurgar-Dawson & Jan Norman from Teesside University , Bea Colley from The Southbank Centre and Fran Golightly and Lesley Shea from Tuned In and Redcar & Cleveland Borough Council for supporting the project. Thanks also go to The Creative Fires Drama Group and Lynn Lawson & Lori York of the Immature Ladies for the cabaret sketches at The Electric Kool-Aid Cabaret plus the musicians, singer-songwriters, bands and guest poets who performed at the Cabarets including: Sara Dennis, Kev Howard, Dominic Nelson-Ashley, Anton Flint, Reece Hanrahan, Chris Stewart, Julie Hogg, Helen Anderson, Curse Pie & The Amplifier, Nobody Girl, Breaking Nerves and Mouses, and everyone who braved The Electric Kool-Aid Cabaret open mic.

Thanks also go to The Danish Arts Foundation, The Dutch Embassy in London and Runoviikko, for their support of the European poets in this project.

Live performance footage of the poets involved in the Intercity Flow Project can be viewed on Youtube.
https://www.youtube.com/channel/UCixPU2Zt_i83wNtZHVR_baw
or just type in 'Intercity Flow'